WITHDRAWN
University of
Illinois Library
at Urbana-Champaign

NUMBER 574

THE ENGLISH EXPERIENCE

ITS RECORD IN EARLY PRINTED BOOKS
PUBLISHED IN FACSIMILE

HEINRICH BULLINGER

ANTIDOTUS AGAINST THE ANABAPTISTES

LONDON, 1548

DA CAPO PRESS
THEATRVM ORBIS TERRARVM LTD.
AMSTERDAM 1973 NEW YORK

The publishers acknowledge their gratitude to
the Syndics of Cambridge University Library
for their permission to reproduce the
Library's copy, Shelfmark: Syn.8.54.129

S.T.C.No. 4059

Collation: A-O^8, p^4

Published in 1973 by

Theatrum Orbis Terrarum Ltd.,
O.Z. Voorburgwal 85, Amsterdam

&

Da Capo Press Inc.
- a subsidiary of Plenum Publishing Corporation
277 West 17th Street, New York N.Y. 1011

Printed in the Netherlands

ISBN 90 221 0574 1

Library of Congress Catalog Card Number:
73-6106

AN·HOL SOME

Antidotus
or counter-
poysen,
agaynst the pestylent
heresye and secte
of the Anabap-
tistes new-
ly trans-
lated
out
of lati
into Englysh by John
Veron, Senonoys.

Pricipiis obsta, sero medicina para
tur
Cū mala per lōgas, inualuere moras
Vidi ego quod fuerat, primo sana
bile vulnus,
Dilatum longæ, damna tuiisse moræ

TO THE

MOST REDOUBTED, prynce Edwarde, by the grace of god, Duke of Somerset, Lorde Protector, of all the kynges maiesties realmes subiectes, and dominions and gouernor of his most roiall persō health, prosperite, ēcrease of honor & heauenly know‑ leg frome god ye father, through out lorde and sauiour Iesu Christ So bett.

HE blesed aposttle saynte Paule, in ye xx. chapiter of the actys, callynge to‑ gether all the seny‑ ours or prestes, at a place and towne called Myletum, dyd spe ake vnto thē after this maner Take ye hede to your selfs, & to al the flock, ouer the which, the holly gost hath

put

A ii.

Against the

put you ouerseers to feade the
congregation of god, which he
purchasyd with his owne blood
for I know this wel, that after
my departynge, shall enter in
greuous wolfes a monge you,
which shall not spare the flock.
And euen of your selfes, shall a
ryse men speakyng peruerse thin
ges, to drawe dyscyples after
them et c. Here, most myghtye
prynce, dyd that chosē & elected
vessell of god, describe most liue
ly, the wicked and peruerse nature, of false & seditious hery-
tyckes, that studye for nowght
elles, but to deuid and seperate
the chnrche, to gette vnto them
disciples, to scater & dissipate
the flocke of þ most bountuous
sheaperde Jesu christe, to sowe
discorde, & teach peruerse thin
ges, et c. Which thynge truely,
dyd

dyd chaunce in the primatyue
churche, euen in the tymes of ẏ
a postelles, to the great hynde-
rance, and let of the gosspell of
Chriſte, for where ſo euer, the
apoſtells and dyſciples of oure
ſauyour, had preachyd ẏ kyngdome of god, and with greate
peane and labour, had brough:
the people, from theyr ſuperſty
tious, and vngodly wayes, in
to the waye of the truthe: there
dyd breake in certayne falſe
prophetes, and falſe a poſtelles
alſo, with there peruerſe and
hypocriticall doctryne, ſubuer-
tynge the myndes of them, that
w̃ ioyfull hartes, had receyued
the glade tidynges of ſaluatiõ
& delyueraunce. Theſe ar they ẏ
for their bealies ſake, dyd, as a
ſtormy & wyndy tẽpeſt, trouble
ẏ peace & vnite of ẏ church ſekig
A iii.   theyr

their owne glori and promotiō, imagynyng alwaies myschefe, in their hartes, how thei coulde gette vnto them selfs, by theyr pestiferous blandiloquēce, and venymed flatterynge tonges, moste shamefully and vntruly, preferryng them selfs, vnto the true apostlles and discyples of our lorde) a perpetuall name & memorye, Agaynst them dyd ÿ apostelles, and speacially saynt Paule (whome we maye right well call the standard bearer, of our Chrysten religion) wrytte very ernestly, callyng them antichristes, false prophetes and pseudoapostills, callyng them euell workmen, enemyes of the crosse and passion of christ, as it appereth more euydently in the actys and in the eppstylls, that they haue wrytten and sent to
sondrye

Anabaptistes

sondrye and many churches, to arme and fense ye flock of christ, agaynst such rauenyng wolfs. Yet notwtstondynge after the departyng of the apostells, that is to saye, after yt god had done hys blessed wyll wt them accordynge to the commen course of nature: these false prophetes, dyd so preualle agaynst the true doctryne of christ, yt in a maner these xii. hunderd yeares, fewe or none durst speake the truthe. For as soone as any man, by ye inspiration and gyft of the holy gost, dyd begyne in those dayes, to preache the gosspell, purely & sincerely, to the great glorye of god and edyfyeng of the church, defending with the swerd of the spiritee, that libertee and frydome, that christ with hys precyous bloode hath purchassyd

Aiiii. vnto

vnto vs (dyd not these hypo-
crites, bryng all the world into
thraldome, puttyng vpõ chriftẽ
menes neckes heauear burdẽs
of humayne traditions and
ceremoniall dreames, thã euer
dyd the Iues beare: whiche as
faynt Augustyne fayth, though
they knew not the tyme of liber
tye, yet notwithstandyng war lo-
ded and burdoned notwith mẽs
presumptions, but with ỹ bur-
dens of the law onely:) by and
by was he, as a falfe heriticke,
or as he that hath kyllyd bothe
father, and mother, most cruely
put to death. In so muche that
the yearthly prynces, whome,
with theyr abhomynabyll dyss-
cimulation, they had gotten on
theyr sede, blyndynge and poy-
fenynge them most subtillye &
craftely, with the golden cuppe
of

A Anabaptiste:

of ye purplyd hore of Babylone, thought, that they dyd a greate sacryfyce vnto god, whan, with all the tirannye that coulde be, for these belys sake, murthered, and persequuted them, whome god had chosē and sent, to shewe vnto them, the waye of truthe & saluation. But blessed be that bontuous lorde, which hath not suffered the prynces, whome by hys diuine prouidence, he hath made & ordoned, to be supreme gouernors of hys church, immedyatly vnder hym (though by ye tyrannicall power of those false prophetes, & antichristes, they ware put, by that superporytye a greate whyle) to erre and bee deceued any lōger, but dyd most mercyfull opē their eyes to loke vpon that comfortable sonne of ryghtuosnes, and lyght of the
A b.   truth

Agaynst the

truthe, þ they myghte, in these
thyk darkenessys of thys wret-
ched worlde, be gydes vnto hys
people, to bryng them out of the
egypte of ignorannycye, and so
leade them through þ parylous
desertes, into þ land of promis-
cion. For the which thynges, we
are all greatly bounde, to gyue
dayly, and hourley, immortall
thākes vnto god, and specially
that, of hys bountuous, & mere
goodnes he hath gyuen vnto vs
such a noble & coragious prince
which now in his tender years,
is so delegentli brought vp, ī all
godlynes & vertuous learning,
that he hereafter, as a nobyll
Salomon, shall w all prudence
and godly wysdome, not onely
shed the blode of them that dyd
shede the innocent bloode, but
also, buylde vp, myghtely, the
temple

¶ Nabaptistes

temple of the liuing god. Which thyng, as dauyd in ẏ olde lawe, so nowe oure moste vyctoryus prynce. Henrye the eyghte, the father of this, oure sofuerayne lorde kyng Edwarde the syxte, wolde had done, if god had not dysposed otherwyse, with hym. But thanckes be to god, that he hath so well, prepared all thynges, before hys death, and that he hath w ẏ tow edgged sworde of the spiritee, cutted a waye alredy, the bushes, thornes and brembles, that shuld had letted the buyldyng of the temple, makyng the ground euen, by abbatynge the pryde of these false apposteles, and puttyng awaye, by litell and litell the rubbyshe, of vngodly traditions and vayne ceremonis. Which thyng wyl be no, smal spurre, vnto our most
   sofuerayne

soueraygne lord, kyng Edward the syxt, to performe and bryng to prosperous, and ioyfull ende, that, which hys louyng father, hath begonne, so godly. And I doubte not, but now (god wyllynge, who neuer forsaketh hys true, and faythfull seruantes, though, to trye theyr fayth, for a tyme and season, suffereth thē to be persequuted) all thynges shall be done to ye glory of god, and greate conforte of ye louing subiectes, of thys noble and florysshyng realme. Among whom (as we may, easely perceyue, by theyr dylygent and greadye comyng to the churches, whan they heare of any sermon, and preachyng) is fallē now a great hunger and thrist, not of thys materyall breaed, and drincke, but of the lyuely worde of god.

but

But alas in stede, of y̆ heauēly
breade, y̆ feadeth to euerlasting
lyfe, they be deluded w̃ blind &
dome ceremones. Which thing,
I trust, not lōg shal cōtynew in
christes churche, where y̆ word
of god, onely should reygne, and
wout y̆ which, purely & sincerly
preached, is no church but a dē
of theues. Excepte I saye these,
vanytes, and pestyferous inuēc-
tions of men: be vtterly banysh-
ed a waye it is more lyke the
carnall temple of the Iues (in
whose Synagoges Moyses, &
the prophetes war reade euery
Sabothe daye, without fayle)
than the church of christe. But
now, sith that it hath pleased
god (whoe lokynge mercyfully
vpon the affliction of his people
hath sent them, a myghtye deli-
uerer) to enhaunce, and make
your

your grace, not onely hygh pro-
tectoꝛ & defendour of this noble
contrey of England, but also a
faithfull ouerſeer, of y̨ buyldyng
of this ſpirituall temple, which
is the church of the lyuyng god,
that, with hys pꝛecious bloode,
he dyd waſhe, frome all ſpote,
blote, and macule, to tryumphe
with hym euerlaſtyng lyfe, in
hys heauenly kyngdome, and y̨
towarde the same buyldyng, as
in the olde lawe, towarde the
ſettyng vp of y̨ tabernacle ſome
men dyd offer gold, ſome ſyluer,
ſome pꝛecyous ſtones, ſome a
gayne dyd offer purple, ſcarlet,
and ſylkes: I thoughte accoꝛ-
dyng, to my pouer abylytye, be
cauſe I coulde, offer none, of y̨
a boue reherced thyngs to offer
at leſt, either ſome vyle gotes:
ſkynes, oꝛ ſome ledde, to couer
thys

Against the

thys spirituall temple, and to
keape, the rayne, and foule wea-
ther, frome that gorgyous and
goodly ornamentes, that other
men, accordyng to their ryche,
& pregnant wytts haue abun-
dantly offered. It is so, that
otherwhyles, for lacke of good
couerture, many fayre, & goodli
places, well & gorgyously trym
med win, and decked plesantly,
with gold, asure, and precious
stones, doo fall in shorte space,
in to great dekaye, by reason of
the rayne ỹ falleth in. Lykwyse
yf a remydye, be not prouyded,
that the churche of god, and ce-
lestyall Jerusalem (whiche is
now almost buyldyd vp agayn,
and through reparated, by our
godly Nehemias) may be fēsed,
against ỹ tempestuous heresis
of the Anabaptistes (whyche,
where

where soeuer the truthe dothe spryng, and begynneth to come abrode, do breake in, infectyng the myndes, of ẏ rude and symple people, with pernitious & detestable opiniōs) surely therof, as afore of the doctryne of ẏ papistes great coueniētes must neades folow. Many townes & cytyes, in Germany and in the Sussynres lande, where, the word of god dyd florish goodly afore, ware cleane subuertyd by thys abhomynable secte. of ẏ Catababtistys (for they ware called anabaptistys, because ẏ they ware autors of rebaptization, or babtizyng agayne, and Catabaptistys, because, ẏ they dyd speake and hold oppynyon, agaynst the baptime of childrē) in so muche, ẏ they had almoste extynguysshed the gospell ther
as it

Anababtistes.

as it is moze euydently shewed, in ye workes of certain famous clerkes of Germanie & Heluetia whiche incomoditie and hurte, that it maye not chance hereafter, in this illustre & victorius realme of England: I haue accordyng to my small learnyng, enterprised, to translate out of latin, into englyshe a litell treatie, that ye famous clerke Henry Bullinger, hathe afore wrytten in the Germanysh tongue, and after, was translatid into latin by Leo Jude, byshope of Tigure agaynste the pestiferous venime of the Anababtistes. Wherein the false and pernicious oppinions of these antichristes, are so clerkely both by scriptures, and also good learnynge, confuted: that it is impossible, where such
B   bookes

bokes, shallbe dilygently peru-
syd, and reade, that this cursyd
heresie shulde take any place.
This shallbe therfore an holsōe
Antidotus or conterpoyson a-
gaynst suche pestilent doctrines
Which J doye, most humbly offer & dedicate vnto your grace,
as vnto hym, that wyll, with all
his myght, and godly power, see
that the worde of god, shallbe e-
uerie where, purely and sincerly preachyd, & that, as a tender
father, wolde be full lothe also, ȳ
any suche erronious doctryne,
shoulde creepe in, to infecte the
louinge, and faithfull subiectes
of thys realme, desyrynge, and
moste mekely besechynge youre
grace, to accepte this my rude
labour, which J haue bestowed
in translating this fyrste boke,
beinge alwayes readie, at your
gracis

Anabaptistes.

graces commandement, to tran
slate the other. iii. as sone, as
god will gyue me grace, who of
his infinite bountuousenesse,
preserue your grace, and al
the noble counseil of Eng
land, long to continue,
in loue, welth, & pros-
peritee, in our lorde
and sauiour Jesu
Christe, to whō
be praise, ho-
nour and
glory,
world without ende.
AMEN.

By your humble and poore
oratour John Verone.

Anabaptistes.

The fyrste, boke agaynste the errours of the Anabaptistes, diuided into dialogues, wherof, the enterloquutors are, Ioiada, who representeth the true christen man & Symon, that taketh the Anabaptistes parte.

How that the worlde, is easily deceiued, and brought to diuision, by fals doctrine.

Ioiada.

That truely, whiche the wise men of the heathen, dyd complayne vpon, saiyng that al mortal men, are exceadyng studiouse, of new thynges, appeareth now to bee true: in so muche that thei doe suffer them selues wilfully to be begyled, and vtterly spoyled, by shameful and abhominable impostours & deceauers (so that

Biii. thei

thei be commended, with hypo­
crisy, and vaine blandiloquence
or flatteryng) although this
thing (if any man, shulde esteme
it after humaine reason) is by
it selfe, bothe myserable, and
full of horrour, yet notwithston­
dyng, it owght most of all, to be
lamented, among vs Christen
men, whiche haue sure and defi­
nite, shorte and moste approued
groundes or foundacions, bothe
of our faithe and of our lyuyng,
wherupon, we may surely leine,
and truste, not suffryng our sel­
ues, thus to be caried about and
tossed to and fro, by suche erro­
neouse persons. But surely, our
synnes, & infidelitie do deserue
it, whiche dooe heare daiely the
worde of god, but do not receiue
it, with a true herte, sekyng, I
can not tell, what other thyng
be­

Anabaptistes.

beside the glorie of god, and true innocencie of lyfe Therfore, are we deserupngly gyuen, in to a reprobate mynde, and in to all kynde of filthinesse and abhomination.   Symon   Lo I see the man, whome I haue loked for, a greate whyll. But is it he, in dede whome I see comynge hetherward, to mete me, or not? I wyll speke vnto hym.
God spede, moste wellbeloued brother. Arte thou not   Ioiada. with whome, I dyd familyarly lyue, in the citie of Lyons. Tell me I praie the, how doest thou? Are all thinges safe, or well? Or what thinge, maketh the, to go, so pensyf, and troublyd in thy mynde?   Ioiada.   As touchinge my selfe, all thynges be well, thankes be vnto god, But it greueth me, that such greate

B iiii   dissen-

Againste the

dissencions, and troubles are among Christen men. And although suche debates and strifes, be neither necessary, nor profitable, for any maner of thyng, yet not withstondyng we dooe see, the poore symple people, to be, on euery syde intangled with the errours of the Anababtistes I am bothe asshamed and sorie also, that suche blyndnesse doeth reigne, that men, can not see, what misfortune doeth folowe, wher soeuer these anababtistes, Doe fixe or set their feate. Surely, it did behoue, that thei shuld haue perceaued, and espied such thynges, & after that thei were ones knowen, to shunne them, & not to swarue, as muche, as the bredthe of a naile from the sure articles of the faithe.   Symon. Tell me I praie ÿ, if thou art a
good

good felow. What harmes, doe these men, go about to doe? for I dare saie and affirme, that I haue not hetherto harde, that thei haue gone about any thyng, that doeth abhorre, from truthe and honesty. In the meane season I know, that many thynges are imputed vnto them, falsely, moreouer that thei be accused, and blamed in many thynges, whiche thei dooe not knowlage them selues, to be gylty in. Ioia. I dooe heare also, that thine eies are blynded by suche men. Which if I doe, bothe heale and opē vnto the, thou wilt geue me thankes, aud remembre this benefyt. Symon. I can not vtterly blame this sorte of men, for yet I haue not harde, that thei haue done any abhomynable thyng. Ioiada. But I wil make

make it, manyfeste vnto the. This secte dyd vtterly subuerte the whole citie of Waltzhountum, and dso cause many of the cytezens, whyche were both good and ryghtfull men, to bee exyled, and to be put from their possessions. Wherfore the gospell (whiche dyd floryshe godly there) was also outrageously extynguysshed. The whiche thyng dyd almoste chaunce, in a citee, called Uormantia. There were Anababtystes in Auguste, in Basile, and in Morania, whiche did affyrme, that Christe was but a prophete, saiyng that the vngodly persones, whiche for theyr vngodlynesse were damned, and the dyuelles also, shulde enioye, the heauenly blesse. In a towne called Sanctogalius, one of them, did smite of

of his owne brothers heade, the
father of heauen (as he sayed)
byddynge hym thus to dooe.
What abhominacion they dooe
commytte, vnder the pretence,
and colour of spirituall matri=
mony, the townes and cittees,
that did oftentymes, greuously
punysshe them, for suche wicked
and abhominable factes, dooe
manifestly shewe and testifie.
And this no man can denay, but
that many of them, do leaue and
forsake their owne wyues and
children, yea all offyce and ho=
nesty beyng casted a syde, dooe
lyue, feade, and fatte them sel=
ues, with other mens labours,
snortyng bothe daie and nyght,
moste slougardely. And where
as, they bee wholely gyuen to
so foule and detestable sen=
sualytee, they dooe interprete
it,

it, to be, the commaundemente, of the heauenly father, persuadyng to women and honeste matrones, that it is impossible for them, to be partakerres of the kyngdome of heauē excepte thei doe abhominabli prostitute, and make common theire owne bodies to all men, sithe that it is, wrytten, that we muste forsake and renounce, to all thynges, ẏ we loue best, and that we ought to suffer all kyndes of infamie, or reproche, for Christ sake, besyde that, that ẏ publicans, and harlottes shalibe preferred, to the ryghtwes, in the kyngdome of heauen, There is no ende, nor measure of ther infydelitie, and falshod, of their liyng and sedition, with the which vices these disobedient persons are on euery syde infectyd. Are these, my Simon

Symon, and other muche greuoser, which I dooe passe ouer here, for the nones, to be callyd vertues: Dooe they seme vnto ẏ yet, to haue done no vnhonest acte? Or canste thou denaye, but that thei haue done these thiges Symon. Truly many thinges are ascribed vnto them falsely and the fame or voyce of the people, dooeth alwayes adde somwhat vnto it. Ioiada. That, which is sayed hetherto, maye be prouyd by sealed letters, and with sure aud infalible witnesses. I haue here wittingly passed ouer theyr abhominable crimes, and haue sayed, a greate deale lesse, than they haue done them selues. Therfore, it greauith me the more, that men are so blynde, that they can not perceiue, nor ponder in their hertes

such

suche thynges. But rather, that a greate sorte of men, dooe embrace those erroneous felowes and rennegates, eauen as, yf they ware fallen, or sent doone from heauen and were saintes amonge mortall men, whiche should preache, none other, but godly & heauëly thinges. Where as thei doe passe, in filthy liuing the Nicolantes, and Valentynians.   Symon. These thiges haue ben hetherto vnknowen vnto me. And I suppose, that they be not all pollutyd, with those filthye abhominationes. But what skyllithe, to them, ÿ are good, what fewe among thë Dooe committe? In the hollie nübre of the apostelles, Judas was a traytour, and yet neuertheleffe was callyd an apostyll. Which (I suppose) coulde not hurte

hurte the other. Moreouer, thei
teache so excellente and godly
thynges, of god, of shunninge
synnes, that I can not perceaue
y̅ they be so wycked, and lewde.
Whan they are takē, they praise
and laude god, they gyue thankes, whan they are put to death
they doe constantly endure and
susteyne, dyeng gladly and wyl-
lynglie.   This thou canste not
denaye my Ioiada, wherfore I
wolde gladly, that thou haddest
hard them as I haue.   Ioiada.
I coulde paraduenture, bringe
here fewe thynges, agaynste the
excepte I knowe well alredye,
all this sorte of men and that
a greate whyle a go. But I am
not ingnoraunte, howe muche
hipocrisye can preuayle, by the
meanes of fraude and deceate.
And as touchynge thyne answere

answere, thou sayest very well in that, that is to wyt, that the wycked facte of fewe, shall not harme the innocent. But thou haste not yet proued, that the cause of the Anababtistes is iust and good, Nor thou canste not shewe one amonge them whiche is not commaculate, and infected with some of these said vices I meane lyenge, falshode, periurie, disobedience, sedicion, idelnes, forsakynge of their wiues and chyldren, turpitude. And though all these vices doe not sticke or cleaue to them al at ones, yet not withstandyng are they every chone pollutid with some of them. That in the mean season I should speake nothyng of their heresie, and sectes, of their pertinacie, of their false & erroneous doctrie. And because thou

thou saiest, that thei speake muche of god. I wolde faine know of the, whether thei, ẏ doe preache the gospell, doe not speake of god also ? Symon. This thei doe greatly denaie. Iola. In this thyng truely thei do wrong and iniury to the preachers of the gospell, testifiyng the contrary to the vniuersall chyrche, that is to saie, denaiyng, that by the gospel truely and syncerely preached the people is taught to put their truste, in the onely and true lyuyng god through Iesu Christe. In so muche that among the enemies of the gospell, it is saied in maner of a prouerbe, that priestes doe preache nothyng elles, but of god and faith onely, beyng offēded, with this preachyng: Man is iustified by faith alone. Sym. Truely lythe matter is so. Ioiad. Now therefore if the Catabaptistes, dooe teache of god and faithe otherwise, surely thei dooe blaspheame god and seduce the people. And if thei doe teache, all one thyng with vs (for so it must be, if thei doe teache ryght, and accordynge to the scriptures) why doe thei therfore separate them selues from vs. Or is not that sufficient, that we teache, sythe that we dooe teache bothe one thyng? Sym. There is one thyng, that ye wyll not teache, that is to saie, that thei, whiche are godly, shulde not sinne at al. And again sinners are not shunned of you Nor ye will not separate your selues, from this pollu'ed, and wicked worlde. Ioiad. We were taught by our sauiour Iesu Christ, that thei, that are whole,

whole, haue no neade of the phi-
sycian, but thei that are sycke.
For the Pharisees dyd obiecte
the same to ÿ disciples of Christ,
saiyng: Why doeth your maister
eate with sinners? furthermore
seyng that no man liueth without synne, not as muche, as the
infaunt of one daie: we owght
not to teache, that men shoulde
not synne at all, but rather to
repent daiely and hourely, and
to beware of sinne, as of a snake,
and that the godly owght not to
dispaire, if thei fall, at any tyme
As for the sinnes, that are committed openly, thei are so exa-
gitate or rebuked by the ministers of the churche. Suche se-
ueritee and extreme grauitee is
vsed in rebukyng, that theyr e-
nemies are wont to saie alredy,
that thei can none other thyng,
            C ii   but

but chide and braule. Agayne,
touchynge abstencion or sepa-
ratyng, we doe not see that euer
Christe did the same, as long as
there was any hope. We doe not
separate our selues, least we become like vnto the Pharisees,
Luc. xviii. Symon. But sinnes
are not forsaken. Joiada. And
that, owght not to bee imputed
to the doctrine, but to them, whi
che doe not folow the teachyng.
The teachyng and doctrine (as
thou grauntest thy selfe) is hol-
some, and in it, nothyng is wan-
tyng or lackynge. What other
thyng doe then, the Catabaptistes, in teachyng the contrary,
but shew theyr pertinacy and a
certaine syngularitee or loue of
them selues, wherby it cometh
to passe, that nothyng but that,
which thei doe them selues pleaseth

ceth them ⁊ As this, is not done, without affection, so it can not be without vice.   Symon. And yet not withstandyng, thou doest not beleue, how deuout they are to god, how full of constancy and grauitee, how feruently thei loue god. Ioiada. I can not beleue, ẏ this deuocion of theirs is without blame, oꝛ is syncere and pure. Foꝛ thei diuide the churche, where no neade is. Foꝛ thou canst not denaie, but that god, is taught by vs truely and faithfully. And that synnes are repꝛehended and rebuked, with great libertee and constauncie. What doe thei therfoꝛe, that we doe not, saue onely, that thei doe separate them selues, frõ other, and are full of obstinacie ⁊ Doeth not Sathã also transfoꝛme him selfe, in to an ãgell of light ⁊

C iii   What

What merueill is therfore, if these impostours or deceitfull persons, can faine them selues, to be sheapeherdes? Thei that doe fisshe, dooe not caste a bare hooke before the fysshes, but doe hyde & couer it, with some pleasaunt and swete baite. And Cato did saie beary well. Whiles the byrder, the byrdes begyleth, The flute alwai swetely pipeth. Nor he is not so foolisshe, as for to set or laye his net before the birdes eies. Did not the bisshop of Rome seduce vs so many yeres, with his peincted hipocrisie, and with his godly and byurne dissimulacion and fraude? But these thynges are gon out of remembraunce, sythe that we doe, so lyghtly addicte or bynde our selues, to these newe impostours, and hipocrites. By what craftes,

craftes, did monkes get so gret richesses, was it not, by flatte‐ryng, and hypocrisie? Was it not, by a feined sanctimony, and holynesse of lyfe? As for that, ỹ thei doe reioyce, when thei are taken, & dye gladly, with pray‐syng and laudyng god, thou do‐est so exaggerate and extoll it, as though these thynges (if thei be done) shulde shewe and proue that their doctrine is true, and that their deedes are good. If thou canst proue that, it shall folowe, that theft and robbery, be iuste and good deedes also. For whan thei be punisshed at the galows, or vpon the whele, thei doe oftentymes suffer it pa‐ciently, & moreouer, doe praise & laude god. Who is so folysshe, to thynke, that he maye thus make his argument? This man
is

is tormented and punisshed, &
yet not withstandynge, dooeth
gyue thankes: ergo, he is a iust
man & holy. If any man, shulde
contende, that this doeth folow,
he muste nedes to graunt also,
that the religion of the Iues, is
moste holy, yea, that their religion onely is true. For no man,
doeth pacientlyer endure, to the
very death, for his religion, thā
the Iues doe. How many heretikes were there (thinkest thou)
which did moste constantly suffer death, testifiyng, wt their o͠ne
blood, that thei had taught the
truthe. Do not oftētime robers
& traitours, which suffer death,
acco2dig to their deseruyng, stif
ly defend their innocencie, to the
last breath? Is therfore y̌ cause
of such an obstacle and desperat
man, iustified before god? Who
doeth

doeth not perceiue, yͤ the farther he is from repentance and confession, so muche the worse he is Symon. It is so as, thou saiest, nor I can not saie, againste it. But this is moste to be lamented, that we, whiche are simple persons, are so tossed and caried to and fro, in so muche, that we can not tel, what is beste to bee doone. The Anababtistes dooe saie, that ye doe erre, and ye saie agayne, that thei be out of the right waie. After my iudgemēt, what misery so euer, or trouble there is, it dooeth come of the priestes. And I dooe thinke, yͭ ther were neuer so troublesome tymes. It were peraduenture better, that I folowyng myne owne mynde, shuld beleue, none of you al, doyng al thinges after myne owne appetite, and witte.

C b   Ioia.

Againste the
Ioiada. Thou shalt not do so, my
Symō, but now, learne by thine
own self what good, doeth come
of the anababtistes & what thou
hast sucked of thē, for thou doest
shew openly, ỹ fruite, that is to
saie, desperacion, and to trust in
thi self, hast thou forgottē, what
god hath commaunded, in Deu
teronomy, saiyng: ye shal not do
euery man, ỹ, which semeth good
vnto you, but that, which ỹ lord
hath commanded. So this phā-
tasticall & new fangled men, do
intangle wt them selues, other
men, & cast thē hedlyng, into all
errours. But ye your selues, are
in the faulte, being the autors of
your one harmes, for such deceit
ful persons, do please you. By &
by, as sone as any cōtencious bo
dy, or some new & vnaccustomed
thing, doeth set forthe his head,
ye come rēning by troppes, & nei

ther warninges nor praiers nor
rebukes can auaile among you.
And whan ye be come into þ bo-
tomles pit of miserie or myschef
ye put þ faulte in the ouerseers,
which do geue you warnyng before, w̄ great fidelitie & trothe.
Whose admonitions if ye would
here, or rather gyue eares to þ
word of god preched vnto you,&
setforth by thē, ye might liue pe
sibly, seig therfore, þ ye cast your
selues through your onefoli, ito
such perplexites ye haue no caus
to ipute it, to þ faithfull sheapherdes, whiche warned you be-
for to beware of such thigs,exhor
ting you to peace, charite, & cō-
cord, but to your oūe selues. Sy.
I haue said þ, which I do thike
yet,þ ther was neuer a more tro
blous world,whoso euer ar þ au
tors of it. Jo. wilt thou know
what þ mattier is? this thig do

stirre vp sedition and tumulltie,
ỹ ye do make euery rascal knaue
minister of gods woꝛd, and that
without any descretion. Besyde
this, thou shewest thiselfe vtter-
lie ignoꝛaunte in histoꝛies, and
vnexperte of woꝛdely thynges,
which doest scarsely knowe, the
actes of one age, noꝛ doeiste not
cõsider farther, than is at hand.
If thou haddest redde the hollie
gospelles & actes of the Apostelles, thou shouldest haue founde
greuouser dissentions, whiche
did rise of the sermons of Chꝛist
and of his apostelles. Finallie
that histoꝛies are full of tumultes, which dyd spꝛyng in tymes
paste, of the false oppinions of
Marcion, Ualentinus, Arrius,
Nestoꝛius Entiches, Donatus,
Pelagius, and other heretikes.
Ther were great tumultes and
rebel-

rebellions, not onely of cities & townes, but also of whole realmes, which wer so great, ẏ ours owght not to be compared with them. Did not bothe christ him selfe, and his apostels gyve warnyng before, that sectes, should aryse? Not because, that for thē we should be amasyd, or despair vtterly, but because, that wee should ẏ more dilygently watch against suche pestiferous sectes not onely to auoyde and shunne them, but to resiste also. Paule doeth apertely saye, Corin. ii. that sectes muste be, that thei which ar faithful, maye be knowen. For euen as a sieue doeth not lese the corne, but clensithe from chaffe and darnell, so the wheate of faithfull men, doeth not perishe by false doctrines, but is tryed, the duste and chaffe being

beeng sifted out. Jhon saieth: Thei wēt out from vs but they ware not of vs, for if thei had bē of vs they trulie shoulde had remayned w̄ vs. Therfor we haue nede of cōstaunce & fortitude or strenght, nor we ought not incōtinētly to forsake the sterne but resist corageously ye waues and stormes. This cōstācy & perseueraunce in the tēpeste is a token that wee are not light, but haue beleued stedfastly and wel. Tentations are signes or proues of faith and of ye truth, and do manifest & shew, how farre we haue beleued to ye true veritee. Sy. Thy meaning is good. Seinge therfore ye thou shewest thyselfe so frendly toward me, & that we haue begōe ones to commone of these thīges: I wil opē my whol mid vnto ye cōfering many and
sondrye

sondry thinges w̄ the, touching
Catabaptisme or oppiniōs of ye
Anababtistes, if so be ye thou hast
time & leasyr to heare me. Ioiada.
I wil gladly obey the and folow
thy mynd. If thou hast any thig
bring it forth, i gods name. Sy
I do meruell, if ther is no good
thing, in the doctrine and oppi
nions of the Anababtistes. For
vnto me, it semeth much other=
wyse, ye is to say, ye ther be many
thinges strongly grounded vpō
the scriptures . Ioiada.
This is all the good, that is
in it, that it cause the a greate
meanye to reade the scriptu=
res, whiche elles wolde but
lyttell, studye in them . As
for that whiche they teache
well, they haue it commune w̄
vs, all the resydue wyll I pro=
ue to bee false and foolyshe.

I

Agaynste the
I am mynded to wryte hereafter agaynst thē wherfore I had noted agaynste their doctrine, certayne conclusions, which the greatest parte of them doe holde For agaynst suche vngodly and blasphemous rēnegates, which doe reiecte the scriptures, which doe affyrme that the deuelles and vngodly or vnfaithfull persones shall obtaine at lenght, the euerlastynge life, doe denaye the god head of Christe, and commite opēly with out all shame suche enorme and abho‑ mynablee actes, what neade is it to wryte? But now wyl set in order my conclusions,

The second treatie or dialoge.

Certayne conclusions agaynste the doctryne of the Anabaptistes, put here affirmatyuely, euen as Ioiada which representeth the faithfull christen man doeth holde them.

Ioiada.

Hat spirite, which repugnith agaynst the meanyng of the spirite that speaketh in the holy scriptures, is not from the father of truthe but from the father of lies the deuell.

None of the Saintes dyd euer by violence or force, set forthe or thruste them selues in to the commune office of a preacher, saue onely whan they ware sente by god, elected and

D.   chosen

chosen, by the apostells and churche.

Christe and the apostels did neuer trouble ye churche for yerthly and temporal thinges, but did chiefly study to nouryshhe the peace and vnitee of al the churches. It appereth therfore, that thei, whiche doe trouble & diuide any churches being wel ordeined & pacified in christ for such thynges, are sedicious, lyers and heretykes.

Thei are to bee counted false prophetes, which not without blasphemy & contempte of the crosse of Christ, do teache, that Christ dyd take awaie onely orygynall synne, affirmyng that thei, which doe fail againe, after that thei be ones purified, and

and clensed by the water of regeneracion, shal not obteine daily remission of their synnes. Thei be also false prophetes, ꝑ doe attribute or adscrib iustification to our owne workes.

Suche are blasphemous agaist the gospell, which doe contēd and affirme that the soules do slepe, after this lyfe not knowyng the nature of the soule, nor the vertue of the resurreccion of Christ.

Rebabtization or babtizing agayne, is not of god, but a new secte deuiding the vnitie of the churche, wherby the most pestiferous, and hurtefull heresie, of Donatus, Inpencius and Pelagius is renewed.

Againste the

The baptime of yong infantes is of god, whiche hath ben & did continue alwaies in the churche, sens the tyme of ye Apostels vnto this tyme, & not lately brought in, by ye byshops.

The office or example of any christen man, cōpelleth not that we should not haue all thynges in cōmon, and nothyng priuate, or to our selues, but doeth moue & enco̅rage vs to care, and see to our houshold, to exercise liberalitee and mercie.

Suche are therfore spoters & macules of christes flocke whiche do forsake their familye and houshold, and beyng addicted or geuen to sedicious fables, do fede them selfes, with other mens laboures, beynge in
this

this thyng, most like vnto mon=
kes, whiche dyd the same, with
their hypocrisye.

The preachers of the gospell,
or ministers of the worde of
god, maye haue goodes of
their own, that is to say howses
and possessions, and moreouer
maye liue of the gospell.

That the Anababtistes ar so
enuious, and do imagine al
wayes and forge calumnia=
cions and lyes, who doeth not
see that it commeth of a hatered
that they haue against the prea=
chers of the gospell, that they
may crepe in and aduaunce thē
selues, extenuatyng therfore the
faythfulnes and fidelitee of the
sheapeheardes before the com=
mons, because they may the bet=
ter

Againste the
ter bee, beleued them selues.

Christen men, whiche are
ryghtfully chosen, may with
out any offēce of god beare
rule, sith that power is the my-
nister of god.

This power is not onely pro
fitable, but also necessarie,
for christen men, therfore
we must be obedient vnto it, ac-
cording to the doctrine of christ,
Peter and Paule.

They which wyll not be obedient to the common ma-
gistrates and rulers, or do
resist against them, doyng them
at any tyme wrong and reproch
fulnes, be not christen men, but
Sanlonites

The

Anabaptistes.

They that refuse to make lauful othes, unto the publike rulers, do manyfestlye against the wyl of god, beyng autours of sedicion, and all dysobedience.

The magistrate and rewler hath the swozde from God, wherwith he may smite the malefactours, and shed the blud of wicked dooers, that both the malefactours may be punysshed and the good and righteous liue surely among the wicked.

The libertie of a chzisten mã is not carnall, they therefoze that in the gospell, do seke carnall thynges and fleshly, are the fellowes of Symon Magus.

We doe not learne in ỹ gospell, that we shuld pay neither rentes nor tithes, but that we ought to paie, our debtes, vnto whom so euer we owe any thyng.

The administraciō of bodily thynges doeth perteine to ỹ magistrates & rulers, whiche doe christen men lyke, whan thei doe after this rule: what so euer ye will that men doe vnto you, doe the same vnto other.

Who so euer kepeth this law & rule, may be, and remayne stil a christen man, though he receiueth bothe rentes and tithes.

These articles haue I, here put generally, because that a great parte of ỹ Anababtistes do hold against them. for I know, ỹ it is mi-

impossible y̆ any man should re=
herse al their errours sith y̆ thei
be ifinit & wout number. For it
is no meruel y̆ thei do fall, from
one errour into an other, seyng,
y̆ thei haue not y̆ same spirite of
truthe. Whiche thyng causeth y̆
so dyuerse & contrary sectes, do
aryse among them, that the one
doeth condemne and excommu=
nicate the other. Symon. If
thou haddest rehersed these arti=
cles before them, thou couldest
not haue done it, wout a quike
and sharpe answere. Ioiada. I
haue proued, my Symon, and
that a greate whyle a go, their
poysoned, and venemed hertes,
and tounges, bothe ready to all
kynd of reuyling, and opprobri=
ousnes, and also more bytter,
than is any worme wode, wher
by any man maye coniecte and
D b knowe

knowe, of what spirite, these phātastical felowes doe speake. But reade thou, the thryde chapiter, of the epystell of saincte James, and thou shalte knowe that I saye true. Symon. I praie the, that thou wylt reherse, out, of this chapiter, the thinges, ỹ moste chyefly, doe for our pourpose, Ioiada. These are the wordes of the apostel: Who is wyse, and endued with knolage amonge you (Let hym shewe, by his good conuersacion, his workes, with a gentell wysdome. If so be, that ye haue bytter enuye and contencion, in your herres, dooe not ye boaste of it, nor be liers againste the truth. For that wisdome, is not connyng from aboue, but yerthly beastelyke, and deauelyshe. For where enuye and contentacion, is, ther
is

Anababtistes.

is incōstancie and wicked workes. But the wisedom whiche is from heauen or from aboue first is chaste, after peasible, meake, tretable, full of mercie, and of good fruites, withoute rache or vnaduised iudgement, and simulacion Hitherto haue we reherſed the wordes of James. Ponder and iudge now, whether the holy Apostle, did not liuelye describe the fashions, and doctrin of the Anababtistes. For what do they els, but ineth and rayle against other men, and that of a despitefull enuye and bitternes, oppressing thē w̄ preiudicial sētence, and iudgemēt ꝭ Sy. They promesse to make an aunswere, before any manne, and to geue a reasonable accoumpt of their doctrine and learnyng.

Moreouer that they wyll suffer
them

them selues patiently to be conuicted of errour. Ioiada. Why dooe they promesse that whiche thei wil neuer perfourm? Thou thy selfe haste knowen manye (to saye the truthe, they doe all of a preiudiciall sentence, stiflie and with great pertinacy, stād in their owne oppinions which saied, that thei ware sufficiētly tawght. dyd knoledge their erroure, and offered them selues to recante, yea and dyd forswere their errour. And by and by as sone, as they ware come, to their complyces or felowes, thei dyd renewe their heresee, and against their othe, and all honestye besyde, dyd obstinatly defende it. What should we doe with suche men? Paule sayeth: Shunne thou an heretyke, after that thou hast warned hym ōes

or

or twyse. Their doctrine therfore, is a certaine pertenax contention, and bitter wysdome, suche as Saynt James doeth descrybe. Symon. In the meane season, they wyll neuer graunt, thy conclusions to be true.

Ioiada. This is, that I saye thei be more styfe & more obstacle thā doeth become any christē men, to be. But thou, that haste lyued, most famylyarly w them knowest wel and perfitly, their foundacions, where vpon they grounde them selues. Symon. No Anababtyst better. Ioiada. I wolde therfore, my Symon. that thou shouldest now dispute agaynst my conclusions as the Anababtistes are wonte to doe but wit hout stomake and contēcion I wyll endeuoure my selfe to corroborate and streingthen them

Againste the
them with holy scriptures, and
to proue that they be true. Sym.
Be it as thou saiest. For I de=
sire to be taughte. Thou
shalte haue me also obe=
diente. so that I may
vnderstande and
perceiue ỹ thy
doctrine and
teachyng
is true.

The third treatie or dialoge.

How that the spirite, which repugneth agaynst the spirite, that speaketh in the scriptures, is not from the father of truth, but from the father of lyes the deuels.

Symon.

Fyrste and formost, I doe meruell, what moueth the, to put this conclusiō where as after myne oppynion and iudgmēt, it is no nede therof. Ioiada. But, it semeth vnto me, to be verye necessarye. For manie of the Anababtistes, doe boaste, I can not tel, what spirite, and father, agaynste the manyfest scriptures. For whan they perceiue them selues, to bee ouer comed, with holye scriptures, and so holden in that they can

can, by no waye escape: by and by, they crye oute, sayeng that the spiritee, teacheth them, an other thyng, that is to saye, eyther to holde theyr peace, or to speake forthe some tryflyng matter, and that they bee, neyther subiecte, ne bound to the litterall sense, or letter. In the which thyng, they dooe no lesse erre, than the Doctoures of the bysshope of Rome, which in matters of fayth, wyll not admyt the scripture to be iudge, but referre al thynges, to theyr interpretation and spiritee. Is not this an hygh blasphemie, that a sinnefull man shoulde presume, to sete hym selfe iudge, ouer the word and wyl of god? asthough he ought not, to bee obedient vnto it, excepte, he were moued, with his owne spiritee, and mocion

cion, to reiecte, or receiue it. I harde ones a papiste doctour, openly in a disputaciō, saie: that we, whiche teache the gospell, dooe teache the truthe, and dyd alowe our teachynge veary well, but that he coulde not, nor durste subscribe vnto it, excepte our teachynge were adprobated and alowed, by the bisshoppe of Rome. Beholde my Symon, what abhominacion is this, that a mortall man shulde take vpon hym, to adprobate, & alowe, the diuine and heauenly veritee: and set hym selfe iudge ouer god? Therfore haue I put this conclusion in the forefront because that the Anababtistes, doe for ẏ moste parte, boast and aduaunce their spirite, vnder such pretence, deceiuyng the simple and rude people. Symon.

E doeth

Doeth not Paule teache this, that the letter, doeth kylle, and the spirit viuifieth or doeth quicken? ii. Corin. iii And Christe doeth saie. Joan. xiiii. The spirite shall teache you all truthe. It is spoken by the lorde also, Hieremy. xxxi. Euery man shall teache no more his neyghbour, saiyng: knowe thou the lorde, but all shall knowe hym, from the lowest, to the hyghest: Finally, John dooeth saie: It is no neede, that euery man dooe teache you, but as the vnction teacheth you of all thinges whiche is true and is no lye. What canst thou saye, agaynst so manyfeste scriptures? Ioiada. To the woordes of Paule I aunsweare thus: That Paul speaketh there of the lawe, whyche kyl-

kylleth vs, as he dooeth declare
moze apertly in the. vii. chap. to
the Romains. And by the spirit,
he vnderstondeth faith, and the
consolacion oz comfozte of the
gospell. That, it is so, the texte
of the whole chapter dooeth testifie. Therefore this place hel-
peth nothyng your errour. For
whan we speake of the woorde
of god we doe not vnderstonde
the bare and deade letter, oz
voyde sonnde of it. but the word
well and truely vnderstonded,
and as it is, in veary dede.
And as, for that, that Chryste
dooeth promesse a spyrite vnto
his dysciples, teachynge them
all thynges, wee dooe admytte
and beleue it. But that spyrite can not bee contrarye to
Chryste, noz teacheth any other
         Eii   thyng

thyng, than Chryst hath taught
Therfore doeth he adde, by and
by: teachyng you, what so euer,
I haue saied vnto you. What
dooe, these thynges perteyne, to
the spirite of the Anabaptistes,
whiche teacheth contrary thyn
ges to the spirite of Christe.
The prophecies of Ioel, and
Hieremye, are vnderstonded of
that same spirite, that Christe
dooeth bothe promesse and geue
to his disciples, as it is euident
ly sene, in the seconde chapiter
of the Actes, and the eyght, to
the Hebrues. Iohn, in his epistell, whan he speaketh of the
vnctyon, dooeth playnely expounde hym selfe, saiynge: I
haue written vnto you, that ye
bee not deceyued (or that, ye
dooe not suffer your selues to be
brought in to errour) whyche
thyng,

thyng, will then come to passe, if ye dooe stedfastely abyde, in the doctrine of the spirite, whiche ye haue harde at the begynnynge, and swarue not at all, from it. The holy ghoste is the spirite of truthe, which canne neither lye, nor repugne against hym selfe, beyng all waies constaunte, vnchaungeable, euery where, lyke vnto hym selfe. Now, no man can denaye, but that the same euerlastyng, vnchaungeable, and holy spirite, hath inspyred the holy scriptures in to holy mens hertes and myndes. Whereby it foloweth necessarily, that the same spirite, which speaketh agaynste the meanyng of the spirite, that dooeth speake and expresse hym selfe in the diuine scriptures, is not of god, but rather an humaine

Againste the
mayne affection, whyche, if it bee styffe, maie bee deseruyngly called, a deauelysshe spyryte, as Chryste dooeth proue agaynste the Jues. John. viii. Or canst thou thynke, in thy mynde, that spirite to bee good, whiche contemneth the cleare, manyfeste, pure and holy scriptures? and when by them, he is conuicted of errour, doeth boste an other spirite, whiche shoulde teache cleane cōtrary thinges? Is not this to despise ẏ spirite of ẏ scriptures, and to repugne against hym? As though our spirit meaneth truely, and the spirit of the scriptures most falsely? Where haue the Anababtistes learned, to set their spirit against ẏ scriptures, yea and preferre hym, to the holy worde of god? Symon.
But

But who hath geuen you this libertee, to iudge al thynges after the litterall sence or letter?
Ioiada. That, we dooe not, as thou doest interprete the letter. But we saie, that the worde of god, conteined in the scriptures of the Bible, is a touche stone, wherby spirites are tried. For what spirite so euer doeth agree with the scriptures, is of god, the father of truthe. And agayne what spirite so euer is contrary to the holy scriptures, is of the dyuelle, the father of lyes. Seyng therfore, that the Spyrite of the Anababtistes, wil not bee ruled by the holy scriptures, but preferreth hym selfe, to the woorde of god (callynge by crafte, the woorde of god, a bare letterre) yea and sette

set him selfe iudge ouer it, he cānot be of god. For if he were of god, he would come to light and speake that same thyng, that the holy ghost doeth speake in al the holy scriptures. But now, sith ỹ he doeth not depende of the scriptures, but will be at his own lybertie, it is a token that it is a craft and subtiltie of the deuell, whiche doeth alwayes scatter & repugne against god. Sy. Thou speakest these thynges mightily and stronglye, but withoute the word of god. And this is your familier custome, to speake many thinges without scriptures. As touching the spirite, what he techeth, I haue brought and alledged places and testimonies oute of the scriptures. But that the spirit ought to be tried by scriptures, or rather mācipated and

bounde

bounde vnto them, and not be at his own libertie, it is thy parte for to proue. Or peraduenture thou dost prefer the creature vnto the creatour. Ioi. What, and yf I should say also: My spirite hath taught me this thyng. What couldest thou do or say vnto me? Sym. But that is not to aunswere. Ioi. Nor ye do not answere sufficiently, when ye bost your spirite, without or agaynst the scriptures. But in this thig we do learne, that whan it pleaseth you, ye vse the scriptures, & agayne whan ye see to be expedeent, ye boaste, aud aduance your spirit. Whan I affirme that the spirite must be tried by the scriptures, I doe not mancipate nor subdue the creatour vnto the creature, but I will that the thynge whiche is vncertaine, be tryed &
proued

proued, by y͢, which is certaine, and that any spirit, be tried, by the holy spirit of god, that is to saie by the scriptures, whether he agreeth with hym self or not. And if he be like euery where vnto him self to be receiued, if not, to be refused & reiected, as false & deceitful. But whan ye speake of the spirite, ye doe vnderstond a bare creature. For your spirit is not the holy ghost, but a carnall affection. Sy. Ye dooe yet without any scriptures of the Bible enhaunce and magnifie, the letter. Jo. Not so, but rather, we here ground our selues, bothe vpon y͢ scriptures of god, and vpon examples. Sy. Shew therfore, y͢ the truthe, muste be tryed, by the scriptures, & not rather w͢ a fre spirit, without scriptures. Jo. By thy wordes, doe
I per=

Anabaptistes.

I perceiue, what thinge doeth begile you, that is, ẏ ye do seuer these.ii.thinges, beyng vnited & inuisebly knitted together, ẏ is to saie, the spirite & the scriptures, which can nor ought to be separated asunder, the one from ẏ other. For whē we name ẏ scriptures, we doe vnderstande ẏ expressed worde of ẏ spirit. For as ẏ voice, or sound of ẏ worde, can in no wise be separated, from ẏ lyuely breth of ẏ liuing creature So ẏ scriptures can not be diuided from ẏ spirit ẏ inspireth thē for ẏ scripture, is ẏ expressed wil of god, but now wil I bryng ẏ testimonies & places wͭ thou requirest, our lord Jesu Christ, vnto whom ẏ heuēly father, did geue witnes from heuen, & who hath receiued the holy ghost, after no measure, did not despise ẏ scriptures, in so muche that he dyd

corroborate all his saipnges, by
them onely, and did commaund
that the Jewes should trye both
his woordes and factes, by the
scriptures. Jhon. v. and Luke
xvi. He biddeth them to lyfte vp
their eyes to Moyses & the prophetes, and not to apparaunte
spirites. He reprouyng also the
Saduceis, did shewe that this
was the cause of their errour, be
cause that they were ignoraunt
in scriptures, or neglected them
Mark. xii. The Apostles (as we
may vnderstand by the booke of
the Actes) did receiue abundãt
ly in the beginyng, the holy gost
& that by a certaine visible tokẽ.
And yet not withstandyng, did
thei not therfore forsake or con-
tẽne ỹ scriptures, nor boste their
spirite against thẽ. But rather
did proue & strengthen all their
sermons,

sermons, with the worde of god preachyng nothyng els, but the pure and playne scriptures. These thynges are euydently proued, by the epistels of Peter. John doeth plainely shewe and teache that the spirites owght, to be tried, whether thei bee of god or not. i. Jo. iiii. Wherby, it is euydent enowgh, that spirites owght to be tried, and that thei be not so free, as the Anababtistes will haue them. And how thei muste bee proued, it is manifestly declared in ẏ place. Paule whiche was rauisshed, in to the thyrde heauen, and dyd learne his gospel of Jesu Christ, beyng hym selfe, the chosen vessel of god, full of the holy ghost, and heauenly wisedome, neuer the lesse before the kyng Agrippa, he doeth testify, that he dyd teache

teache nothyng beside Moises,
and the prophetes. Act. xxvi. In
the epistell to the Galathians,
ÿ first chapter, he saieth thus: if
I, or an angel of heauen, shulde
preach vnto you, any other thig,
then ye haue harde, let it be ana-
thema, or acursed, He also warnyng and teachyng Tymothe,
that he shoulde beware of false
and erroneous doctrines, dyd
directe and sende hym, to the re-
dyng of scriptures. But reade
thou the iii. chapiter of the seconde epistell, to Tymothe, and
it shall appere, what we owght
to iudge and thynke of the Anababtistes secte, what of the spirite, and of the scriptures. Sy.
That place, is knowen well e-
nowghe, and I am almost persuaded. But this vexed my
mynde, that Paule saieth that
a spi-

a spirituall man, iudgeth all thynges, but he is iudged of no body. Ioiada. I longe to knowe of the, of what spirite, Paule doeth speake there. Symon. But I haue leauer to heare it, of the Ioiada. Considre the woordes, ẏ go before. For he saieth thus: We haue not receiued the spirit of the world, but the spirit, whiche is of god, that we may know what thynges, haue ben geuen vnto vs by Chryst. Symon. But to what purpose did Paul speke here, of the holy ghost. Ioiada. I aske of the, wheather ẏ same selfe spirite dyd not inspyre the scriptures. Symon. Truely, that same selfe spirite. Ioiada. Seyng therfore, that it is all one, and bothe the same spirite, that Paule speaketh of here, and that whiche speaketh in the scrip-

scriptures, haue I not proued, that Paule, by a spirituall man did not vnderstond hym, which boasteth, I can not tell, what spirite, despisyng in the meane season the scriptures, but suche a spirituall man, as is and will be ruled and gouerned by the holy ghost, that waie, that he sheweth and expresseth hym selfe, in the holy scriptures. He therfore that striueth againste the holy scripture and inspiracyon of the holy ghost, can not bee that spirituall man, whome Paule doeth speke of. Now, if he be not spirituall, he can not iudge, but he muste be iudged. The Anabaptistes therfore can iudge nothyng, but ought to bee iudged and tryed, by the worde of god. Hathe not here the spirite of the Anabaptistes lost bothe his winges

ges ⁂ But I do remembre other
ii. places, whiche dooe vtterly
stoppe the mouthes of the Cata=
babtistes. The first is, in the. x.
chapiter of the Actes, touchyng
Corneltus the centurion, which
although he was elected by god,
yet not withstandyng, beyng so
tawght by the angell, did sende
messangers, to fetche Peter, ẏ
he migh heare by hym, the preach-
ig of our sauiour Iesu christ.
If that, the spirite should disanulle and abolissche the scriptu=
res, it shulde folow, ẏ this out=
warde preachyng and such like
thinges, wer done in vaine. The
other is in the.xvi. chapiter, con
cernyng the Thessaloniens, whi
che after that thei had harde the
preachyng of Paule, dyd daily
seke and serche the scriptures,
to knowe, wheather Paule dyd
        F   teache

Againste the

teache true or not. Which thing, thei wolde not haue done, if the spirites shoulde not be tried by the scriptures wherefore what so euer the Anababtistes dooe teache concernyng this thynge, is false and erroneous, and not vnlike vnto the errour of Montanus. Sym. what monstruous thyng is ỹ? Ioiada. This Montanus about. xiii. hundred yeres a go, was a great heretike, who did almost speake of the spirite, as the Anababtistes dooe. For thei do cal in again, the old & abolisshed errours, as it shall appere hereafter. Sym. Go forth I praie ỹ, and let vs discusse the argumentes of the second conclusion. For I can not beleue that none of the saynttes (whiche thyng thou doest affirme stifly) did thruste them selues, into the

the office of common preachers, excepte thei were called. What other thyng is this, but (as the bisshop of Rome hath done in times paste) to hyde the truthe frome the commons, that none, saue onely thei, that are learned, dare speake and talke of it? Where as, not withstandynge, god did manifest him self to the littell ones and not to the wise. Mathew. xi. Ioiada. I will doe it gladly, but I wil first confute that, which thou bryngest of the learned, & of the symple. For it is not conuenient, that I shulde passe ouer these thynges vnspoken, sithe that therwith ye doe blynd the eyes of the simple and rude people.

Againste the

The. iiii. treatie, or dialoge touchynge simplicitee and erudicion.

Symon.

IS this, to blynde the eies of the symple, & rude people, Chryste hym selfe, did saie so, when he gaue thankes vnto his father, because ỹ he hath reuelated & shewed such high, godly and diuine misteries, not to the wises, but to the litell ones, & to the simple. Ma. xi. And againe, he did not chose learned men but simple and idiots, to be his apostels. i. Cor. i. Therfore we haue no neede of great learnyng, but the simpler that any man is, the more apte is he, to this office. Ioiada. It is manifeste and euident, that ye vnderstonde not the woordes of

of Chryst. For if by the symple,
he shulde vnderstond them, that
lacke wisedome and learnynge
(for so ye expounde the wordes
of Christ) truely no man shulde
be more apt, than fooles and di-
serdes, whiche be in dede ignoraunt in all maner of thinges.
But every man dooeth see, that
it is against al reason, to thinke
any such thyng. Therfore Christ
vnderstondeth by simplicitee an
other thyng. Symon. Tell you
what it is. Ioiada. He is called a symple man, not he that is
without witte, without reason
and wisdome, but he whiche is
playne and sincere, and without
fraude, he whiche is good, and
true inwardly in his herte, beynge without crafte and deceit.
Elles it woulde come to passe,
that every man shoulde defende
　　　　　f iii　　　his

his errour, by ignorancie. Whiche thyng, what coulde be elles, but a carnall malice or libertee, wherby euery man woulde begynne and goe about, to boaste and sette forthe his ignorancie, and therewith to defende his errours? Who did euer see, suche temerarious audacitee, as these shamefull rennegates dooe vse: that with theyr ignorancie and rudenesse dare defende any thynge? By ignorauncy truely, errours are detected, and not confyrmed. Symon. Yet, the apostels were ignoraunt and vnlearned, nor we dooe not reade, that Chryst did choose any that were learned. Ioiada. Truely thei were endued with such simplicitee, as we haue spoken of afore. But they were not vnlerned and ignoraunt. For they were

were familiarly conuersant with
Chryste, aboue three yeares, w̄
Christ, I say, in whom are, all y͡
treasures wisdō of & knowlage,
yea, which is hym self, y͡ eternal
wisedome of y͡ heauenly father.
Of this fountaine drāke they a-
bundantly, by this maister, wer
thei instituted and tawght, and
at lengthe were so endued, and
illuminated with the holy ghost
that they were cunnynge in all
tonges & scriptures. That may
be sene, bothe by their writyngs
and also by theyr actes. As for
that, that thou denaiest, y͡ christ
did call none, whiche were learned, doest thou not repugne here
agaist y͡ manifest truthe=Paull
was ercedyngly well lerned.
Barnabas, Gamaliell, Nicode-
demus, & Apollo y Alexandrian
were great clerkes. That in the
F iiii   meane

meane season, I shulde passe o-
uer all the other, that is to saie,
Moises, whiche was learned in
al the sciences of the Egipcians
Steauen, Esaie, Timothe, loke
better vpon the xiii. chap. of the
first epistel, to the Corinthians,
and vpon the first chap. of the e-
pistell, to Titus, and thou shalt
fynde what erudicion and learnynge an ouerseer or bisshoppe
ought to haue. Therfore, these
arrogant & presumptuous Ana
babtistes, can not excuse nor defende, their impudent ignorancie, by simplenes, but that it is
alredy manifest vnto the worlde
ÿ they are geuen into a reprobate sence, as thei, that be not a-
shamed, to boast, and to set forth
vnto all men, their ignorancie,
in stede of good learnynge, as
though children, do not smel already

redy, their craft & subtiltee. But in ẏ meane seasõ, no man ought thus, to interprete our saiynges as though we shuld speake here, of them, that are falsely, called learned men. For we speake of such, as haue ben taught, by god & to the glory of god. Of whom, there were many, in the primitiue churche, as Pãtonus, Tertulian, Cyprian, Lactantius, Augustine, and many other.

Sy Thou speakeste, with good reasõ. For we ought not to think that Chryste did commend such simplicitee, wherby the vnconnynger that a man is, the bolder he shoulde be. As many, whiche though thei can scarsely reade ẏ vulgare tonge, yet not withstandyng, doe without shame, ingerate & thrust them selues, in to ẏ office of preachers, stamering

f b   most

most foolysshely in the common pulpit, But because thei shulde not be founde to bee ignoraunt, in some thyng: they begyn first to excuse their ignorancie, with such woordes. Be not ye offended, o bretherne, that I am ignorant and vnlearned. For the father, doeth manifest hym selfe to the symple and vnlerned. Finally, seyng that Christe, doeth promesse, to his disciples suche wisedome, and eloquence, that their aduersaries, should not be able to withstond it (where as, on the contrary part, these men doe recken their ignorancie, to be a glorious thyng vnto them) I mai easily perceiue, that these are not suche simple persons as Chryste doeth speake of, but rather such, as doe clothe them selues, in sheapes skinnes, faining them

Anabaptistes.

them selues, to be sheapes, but inwardely, within theyr hertes, are rauenyng wolues. But now, I praye the, to take that awaye quickely, whyche offendeth me in the seconde conclusion.

The. v. treatie or dialoge.
Of the vocacion and office of preachers, against them, that ingerate them selues beynge vncalled.

Ioiada.

As for that, that thou gatherest, by this cōclusion, ẏ so, it shulde not, be laufull for euery man, to speake and talke of god, thou goest far out of the waie, and doest not vnderstond my saiynges. I speake of common preachyng, and not of priuate communicacion or talke. For he that taketh vpon hym to be a common preacher, not being called, doeth rauen as he, that maketh hym selfe, by his owne authoritee, a kyng or gouernour, makyng & callyng together a particuler Senate or coun-

counseill, & beginneth thus, of his owne heade, to rule and administrate the common welthe, commaunding, and forbiddyng what so euer pleaseth him. Truly, no man, can dooe this, but ẏ he shalbe accused, not onely of folishenesse & disobedience, but also of tumultee, and high treason. Elles, we do not denaie, but ẏ euery man maie talke of god, yea & maie synge of him, accordyng to ẏ doctrine of Paule. iiii Ephesy. And the more, ẏ it is done, the better we alow it. But to separate him self frō ẏ church to seke woods & corners, & there to assemble a company, to institute & ordein sectes and to take vpon them selues, beyng vncalled, & vnsent, the office of preachers: not onely, it hath no example, in ẏ holy scriptures, but hath

hath ben iudged and condem=
ned alwais as heretikall. But
we will now, corroborate and
strength these saiynges, with ho
ly scripture. In the epist. to the
Rom. x. chap. Paule teacheth af
ter this maner: who so euer calleth vpon the name of the lorde,
shalbe saued. But how can thei
call vpon hym, in whome they
haue not beleued ? and how shal
thei beleue in hym, of whom thei
haue not harde ? And how can
they heare without a preacher ?
And agayne how shal thei preache, except thei be sent? By these
wordes of Paule, we maie perceiue, that sendyng is veary necessary, whiche doeth not equally pertaine vnto all men. For
Paule. i. Corin. xii saieth, that
there be many giftes. And eauen as the body is one thynge,
and

and hath many lymmes, which
lymmes, though thei belong all
to one body, yet neuerthelesse,
haue not all owne offyce, in the
body, so it is in the churche, and
misticall body of Chryste. God
dyd putte and ordeyne some, in
the churche, to be apostels, some
to bee prophetes and interpre-
tours of scriptures, some to bee
teachers, some to bee potestates
and rulers, summe to haue the
giftes of healynge, summe to
minister to the poore, summe
to gouerne, and summe agayne
to haue the knowledge of tonges. If so bee, that the offyce
of teachyng, shulde equally perteine vnto al men: Paul would
haue sayed, that god hadde ordeyned all, to bee prophettes,
and teachers, but he sayeth: he
hathe ordeyned summe to bee
apostels,

apostels. &c. Why dare then the
Anababtistes presume so much,
as for to set them selues forthe,
by their own autoritee, to prea=
che & to teach, againste the doc=
trine of Paule Hebrues. v. No
man (saieth he) doeth vsurpe, or
presumptuousli take that honor
vnto hym selfe, but he, which is
called by god, as Aarō, so christ
did not glorifie hym selfe to bee
made bisschoppe, but he that sai=
ed vnto hym. Thou art my sonne
and to daye haue I begotten
the. And in an other place:
Thou arte a priest for euer, af=
ter the order of Melchysedecke.
After this maner dooeth John
Babtiste, testifye of the missi=
on and sendynge of Chryste in
the fyrste, and thyrde chapiter
of John. And of his owne sen=
dyng, doeth he hym selfe speake,
in

in the. i. cha. of John, saiynge:
There was a man sente by god,
whose name was John when he
was also asked, by what autho=
ritee he did teache and babtize,
he did bryng forthe out of Esaie
and Malachie, a testimony and
witnesse of his mission and sen=
dyng. So the Apostelles were
bothe called and sent, as it ap=
peareth, by the x. and. xxviii. of
Mathew, by ẏ last of Mar. and.
xx. of Io. Paule doeth testifie in
ẏ begynnyng of his epistels, and
specially in the epistell to ẏ Ga-
lathiãs, that he was called. In
the. xiii. of the Act. he with Barnabas, is segregated by the holy ghost and sent to preache. In
Moises also, & in all the prophetes their mission and sendyng is
manifested. But agaynst them
that dooe renne, beyng not cal=

G   led

Againste the
called, and without sendyng doe
preache, in the. xxiii. of Hieremy, the lorde speaketh thus
Thei did renne, but I sent them
not. Therfore, I do thynke, that
this conclusion is sufficiently
proued, and that it is manifeste
enough, that the Anababtistes
dooe not in this thyng, behaue
them selues wel and godly, whiche, thowgh thei be not called,
Do ingerate and thrust them selues, in to the office of preachers
Which thyng (as we doe reade)
was neuer done by none of the
Saintes. Symon. All this that
thou hast brought, dooeth nothyng agaynste the Anababtistes for thei saie, that thei bee
sent, by the father, and by the holy ghost. Ioiada. To what thing
or for what pourpose. Symo
To teache the truthe, to preache
of

of god, and to rebuke synne.
Ioiada. It is proued before (as thou thy selfe haste graunted) that we dooe, the same thynge, in those places, where the gospell is preached. What neede haue we then of this mission, and sendynge of the Anababtistes. To these places where the gospell is preached, god dooeth not sende men to plante and set errours, to moue sedicion, and to teache contrary doctrine, to the truthe, to separat and make diuision in the churche. But the Anababtistes, dooe all these thynges, therfore, they bee not sente by god. For god, is not the god of dyssencion, but of peace, and concorde, .i. Corin. xiiii. Symon. Thei saie alwaies, that they bee sente of god.
Ioiada. Thei doe saie so in dede,

but not truely. For Sathan can
transforme and transfigurate
hym selfe into an angell of light
ii. Corin. xi. but he is not therfore a good aungell. Symon.
Is it not written in the. iii. cha.
of John, that he, which is of god
speaketh the woorde of god? the
Anababtistes dooe preache the
worde of god, therfore, they bee
sent of god. Ioiada Arrius
dyd preache the worde of god.
That is to saye, the father is
greater than I am, ergo he was
sent by god. Symon. Not so.
  Ioiada. Is not this the worde
of god, the father, is greatter
than I am? Symon. He dyd
preache the worde of god beyng
falsely vnderstonded, wrethyng
and wrastynge the scriptures,
ergo he was not sent, of god
Ioiada. The Anababtistes dooe
the

the same, therefore they bee not sent by god, though, they dooe neuer so muche boast and crake, that thei doe preache the truthe and worde of god. Which thing, all the heretikes dyd before, and Sathan also dooeth vsurpe the worde of god, Mathew. iiii. but it foloweth not, that he is sent by god. That saiynge, whyche thou hast brought out of the. iii. chapiter of John, perteyneth onely to Chryste, who because y̆ he was come frome god, hath perfite knowlage, of diuine and heauenly thynges. Which thing John Babtiste, goeth about to proue to his disciples. Symon. The Anababtistes doe saie, that ye doe deprauate the scriptures. Ioiada. It skylleth not what they saie, whyche are nothynge shamed to lye, as it shall ma‑

G iii nifestly

nyfestly appere hereafter. For
sythe that by this authoritee taken out of the. iii chapter of
John, and applied to Chryste
alone, thei ascribe vnto them
selues that, which belongeth to
Chryste onely: who dooeth not
perceiue and see, that thei be e-
nemies of the truthe. We know,
what sklanderous wordes thei
doe vomite out, and speake a-
gaynste vs, callyng vs theues,
robbers, Antichristes, false prophetes, and seductors. We doe
impute this to the weakenesse
of the flesshe, and forbeare for
Chrystes sake. We might cleare
our selues, if nede were, & proue
that thei doe beelye vs. But so
thei haue nede to proue, ӯ thei be
sent of god, by other thinges thē
by sklanderous wordes and rai-
linges. Sy. I can not saie none
other

Anabaptistes.

other, but that I haue harde them saie, that thei are sent of god. Ioiada. No doubt there is, but that thei be ignoraunt, and know not, whiche waie, god doeth call, & what are the tokens and signes of vocacion and sendyng. For thei, that are called & sent of god, are manifested by certaine tokens and signes whiche doe folow, that it maie appeare, that thei be truely called and sent either by miracles, or by manifest vocacion and sendynge, but specially by dexteritee or apteneſſe, integreted of lyfe, constauncy and stedfastnesse, erudicion and learnynge, woorthy suche sendynge and vocacion. Symon. what, and if ye dooe faine all this, without scriptures? Ioiada. I wyll proue all, that I haue

G iiii   saied

saied by the worde of god. A littell afore, that Chryste did departe from his apostels, he did sende them, vnto the worlde, to preache the gospel, vnto all cretures, but before, ẏ thei shoulde take in honde this offyce, they shulde tary a while in Hierusalem till they were endued with grace frome aboue. For he dyd promise vnto them, to sende the promised spirit and comfortour of the father vpon them. And after, that thei had ones receiued the holy ghost, with it, thei did receiue, the knowlage of all sciences, speches, & tongues. Luc. xxiiii. Act. ii. whan Moises dyd drawbacke, and did bryng many excuses, knowledgyng hym selfe, to bee without vtterance, vneloquent, chyldisshe, and vnmete for that offyce, that god would woulde haue sent hym to: the lord, did promise, that he would be in his mouth, as, he dyd also promise to his apostelles, suche mouth and wisedome, that no man shoulde bee able to resyste agaynste it. Mathew. x. Paule wrytynge to Tymothe and Titus, concernyng the election of bysshoppes, requireth such one, as, is apte to teache, able to exhorte with wholsome doctrine, whyche can reuycte, and confounde them, that resyste and withsaie the truthe. i. Timothe, iii. Titus. i. There Paule doeth forbydde, that none of them, whyche were newly conuerted, shoulde be admitted to the office of a preacher. Hetherto, haue I brought places and testimonies out of the scriptures, touchyng the learnyng, that ought to be in an ouerseer or bysshop. Now shall we heare, what the scriptures doe testifie and witnesse concernyng the miracles of them, that are sent. We dooe therfore alleage here the wonders, that Moyses did shewe, in Egypte and other innumerable signes, and tokens, that bee written in the Actes, the manifeste imposicion of handes, and that thei dyd receiue the holy ghost visebly. Moreouer that thei, whiche be sent, ought to be laufully elected and chosen by a common assent, we dooe bryng the first chapiter of the Actes, vpon the election of Mathias the vii. and. xiii. of the Actes vpon the election of Steuen Paule and Barnabas. The. xiii. chap. also of the Actes doeth manifestly shewe, that Paule and Barnabas

nabas, when thei had created, thorow all the churches by a generall election priestes or seniours, laiyng their handes vpon them, and had made theyr praiers with fastyng, did committe them vnto the lorde, in whome thei had beleued. Now thou seest, my Symon, that in ye times of the Apostels. euery man dyd not rasshely aduaunce nor sette for the hym selfe to preache. For if it hadde ben so, what shoulde haue neaded any election, and imposicion of handes? But election was made after praiers & fastyng. The same is also written in the epistell to Titus. Sy. What, & if thou fyndest all such thynges, among the Anababtistes? Jo. Not ye lesse iote, of al ye aboue rehersed thiges, ergo thei are not set by god, but sensualitee and

and ipmpudent boldenesse, dyd
impell & moue them. For, what
myracles doe thei? except, these
are, to be called miracles, that
they, with their pernicious doc=
trine, dooe brynge men, out of
their right, and godly minde, in
to starke madnesse, or, hat thei,
make the gammons, and legges
of bakon, hangynge in the lar=
ders, of the symple and poore
people, inuisible? What lear=
nynge, should we loke for, where
rudenes, and (as thei do speake
them selues) simplicitee, is ta=
ken for hyghe rudicion? I dooe
passe ouer here, many of them,
whiche can scarcely reade, yea
and what wyll ye saie of them,
ẏ can reade no maner of thyng
Are not these, ẏ neophites (by ẏ
neophites, I meane not onely
them, that are newly conuerted,
but

but such as doe lacke learnyng)
that Paule do reiecte. But thei
promote them, that by all their
lyues tyme, did neuer reade the
Bybles, hauyng onely in readinesse, certaine sentences, not vnderstonded, which beyng, either
plucked out, of al partes of scrip
ture, or stolen, or els borowed, of
their gydes & leaders, thei dooe
wrethe, wrast & turne to conten
cion, w all maledicence, & reui-
lyng. And so, stondyng among
the simple people, haue alwais
in their tonges endes, y̌ father
of heauen and the spirite. What
name, my Symon, maie conue-
niently, be geuen vnto them? I
maie not call them apostels, for
thei are not sent, by god. Again,
thei do not preache wher nothin
hath ben yet preached of god but
where y̌ people, hath ben a long
sea-

Againste the

season, & with the great labour of the true and faithfull ministers, taught the waie of truthe there doe thei breake in, destroiyng, peruertyng, &, as a storme or tempest, stirryng vp, all thinges, makyng the commons so perplexed, and doubtfull, that thei know neither ende nor begynnyng. If any man, shoulde call them prophetes and expositours of the scriptures, it were none other thyng, but to call a filthy swine, an excellent & cunning Musician. For thei are ignorant in al maner of tongues, in so muche, that thei doe contemne them, being content with ye bulgare tongue onely, If thou callest thē doctours, they know nothynge lesse, than the right waie and trade of teachyng. Besides, that thei want the truthe,

which

Anababtistes.

whiche is chiefly required in a teacher. But paraduenture, thei will be called bishops and sheapherdes. Why do ẏ lacke then al suche excellent giftes, as Paule requireth in a teacher oʒ bishop In so much that thei be vnlearned, striuers, contencious and rude neophites ⁊ Briefly they haue nothyng, that perteine to ẏ office of a teacher. Wherby any man maie perceiue, that the Anababtistes, are suche, as doe send them selues, beyng perplexed, sedicious debatefull, ⁊ ambitious heretykes. Sy. Thei be bothe chosen, and sent. Ioi. By whome ⁊ Sy. By their church Moʒeouer, one bʒother, dooeth lai his hand vpõ ẏ other, geuing hym ful power ⁊ autoʒitee. Io. This sendyng, ⁊ election, maketh me, to remẽbʒe ẏ bisihop of
Rome

Againste the
Rome, for after, that the bisshop of Rome, dyd ones get & pourchasse vnto hym selfe, thorowgh disobedience, tirannie and pernicious crafte, suche great power: by and by, dyd he promote to bisshoprykes, euery mule keper, bawdes and blody souldyours But, who did teache them, to seuer and diuide the churche, beynge vnited, and glued with faithe, and charitee ? seynge that there is but one God, one faythe one babtyme, and one churche ? Who hathe sent the authours of this secte, to make and congregate a new churche? Truely, amulacion, enuy, strife, contencion, auaryce, ambicion, and stisse pertinacy. I could wel and sufficiently proue all these thynges. except, I shoulde here wittyngly, spare some people.
Their

Anabaptistes.

Their Churche therfore, is not the Churche of God, but a certayne secte, and congregacion of styffenecked and disobedient people, among whom, there is no moze iust election, then is in the company of rebelles & traytours, whiche forsakyng their owne prince or gouernour, doo retchely, & without aduisement chuse, thys man or that man, to be their Capitayne. But let vs graunt, that it is a Church, yet notwithstandyng, they erre in election, whiche is not vsed among them, accordyng to the preceptes of the apostle, Donatus, dyd gather a particuler Church. Donatus lykewyse, & bothe in Affrica. And yet not withstandynge, none of theim both, was called or sent by god. And their Churche also, were

no Churches, but conuenticles
or assembles of Heretikes.
Symon What thynkest thou by
the saiyng of S. Paule .i. Corin.
xiiii. where he doth geue free libertie, vnto all men to preache,
or interprete the Scriptures.
Ioiada. I am of the same selfe o-
pinion, that Paule is: Two or
thre (sayth he) may speake in
the church: Let the other heare
and iudge. Finally, if it be reuelated to an other syttyng by,
let the other holde his peace.

And by and by it followeth:
For ye may al prophecy, one after another, that all may learne
and haue consolacion. Symon.
By these wordes, it appeareth.
that Paule dothe not geue libertie to euery man, to preache
what he listeth, whē he nameth
ii. or .iii. and byddeth the other
to

Anababtistes.

to heare, & to geue attendance to that that the Prophetes (in the newe Testament, suche, as do expounde the scriptures are called Prophetes) do expounde and set furthe out of the scriptures. Nor he doth not gyue lysence to the hearers, to interrupte the sermons of the Prophetes, excepte it be, when any thyng is lefte or peruersly expounded by the Prophet, or interpretor. By this, it foloweth, that it is not semely ne comely, that any mā shuld interrupt, if the truthe be sufficiētly enucleated & shewed, muche lesse, that any man shoulde, vnder suche pretence and colour sewe in, or bring in his errors. I doo see & perceiue, that the effecte of the matter doeth consist, in thys thyng: If it be necessary, if any

H.ii. thyng

thyng be omitted and lefte, by
them that are Prophetes, that
oughte not to bee omitted, or
whiche beynge lefte, maye dooe
harme: and agayne, which being shewed, may edifi the chur=
che, that then it may be shewed
vnto them, by any mā, but that,
with al sobrenesse and charitie.
If nothing be wanting or lack=
ynge, all the audience to holde
their ptace. Ioiada. Thou takest
the ryght sense of it. For it fo=
loweth by and by: The spirite of
the Prophetes, is subiect to the
Prophetes. For God is not the
auctor of confusiō, but of peace.
The Holy ghost doth not breake
furth rashely, ⁊ with affection
and strpfe, but is treatable: nor
he dooeth not styffely contende
for euery lyght matter, but suf=
fereth him self to be instructed,
and

and taughte: ꝛ so geueth easely place, to him that hathe better vnderstandyng. But the Anababtistes are farre from al such thinges, boastyng neuertheleſſe a spirit, but as Judas did boaſt his Apostleship: sayut James, dyd not without a cause, warne vs, saiyng: Let not many maſters be among you, knowynge that we shall receyue greatter dampnaciō oꝛ iudgement, that is to say: we that are teachers.

Symon. But here thou haſte bꝛought me into a greter dout: Foꝛ now Jaſke the: Whether of theym two is greatter, the Pꝛophet. vnto whom the spirit is subiect, oꝛ the spirit? If thou sayeſt, that man is gretter, then the spirite, beware that thou doeſt not attribute to much to a moꝛtall and frayle man. If the spirite

spirite is hygher, how can that thyng, which is gretter, be subiecte to a thyng, that is lesse. If so bee, that thou preferrest the spirite vnto men, & agayne wyll haue the saiyng of Paule to be true, I do not perceine, by what reason it can stande. Or howe can a man be greatter, then the Spirite, whiche maketh hym a Prophet? Ioiada. Thou dooest aske righte well this question. But it is to be noted, that Paul doeth not here take the spirite for the holy ghost, whiche is the thyrde persone in trinitie, but for the gyfte & operacion of the spirite of God. The sense and meanyng of this place, is therfore, that the gyfte of prophecy, is so in the power of the Prophet, that hath it, that he maye bothe speake, & holde his peace,
in the

in the congregacion of the sayntes, when, and as long, as it is expedient for the hearers. For they are not so instructed and moued, with the spirit, as mad, and phantasticall men are, that they shoulde all cry out at once, with an vnsemely clamor, murmuryng one agaynst another, with a debatefull contencion & stryfe: For so, one coulde not vnderstande another. The spirite of God is gentle, treatable, and peasable, not stirrynge or mouyng any man to contenciō, and debate, but to peace and vnytie. Wherfore he sayeth: ye may Prophecy all, one after another. To the which exposiciō, Theophilactus, agreith, interpretynge this place, after thys maner: The spirite, that is to say, the grace of the holy ghost, which

Against the which is in thee, the operacion or workyng, that hath inuaded thee, is subiecte to the gyfte or grace of another man, which is moued to Prophecy, that is to say, do the geue place & hearing. But now, if thou be so pleased, let vs go aboute the thirde Conclusion.
Symon. I am well content, begynne thou.
✠

Anabaptistes.

The .vi. Treatyse or Dialogue.

Of the Unitie of the Churche, agaynst the Sectes of the Anabaptistes.

Ioiada.

I Thynke, that thou wylt say nothyng agaynst the thyrd conclusion: For, what canne be sayde more truly, then that Christ, and his Apostles, dyd alwayes congregate, or assemble the Churche, and that thei dyd neuer tumultuate or moue sedision, for outwarde and temporall thynges. Or is there any man, that can say the contrarye? Symon. I wyl shew hym vnto the by & by, that is to say, Christ, whiche dothe saye: I am come, not to bring peace, but the swoorde.

H. b.   Ioiada.

Ioiada. Thou dooest writhe and wrest the wordes of Christ: For he speaketh not these wordes of his Churche, that they shoulde disagree within themselues, as the Anabaptistes do moue tumulte, in those churches, where Christ and the Gospell is preached sincerely, but doth expres the nature of the infidels, whiche doo persecute the faythfull. For, whersoeuer Christ is preched, they that are godly, do receyue and embrace him gladly: and they that are vngodly, doo bothe let and persecute Christ and his Disciples. Now Christ doth cal this discenciõ a sword: which sworde is not among the godly in the Churche: but the infidels do vse it agaynst them that ar godly. Dothe not Esaie say, that there is no peace to the vngodly

vngodly. The cognisaunce or badge of them that ar godly, is Charitie, Peace, and Concord. Wherfore, the Lorde, dothe call them, that be peasable, or loue peace, blessed, and chyldren of God. Mat. v. Symon. I do easely graunte, that peace aud vnitie ought to be, in the Church. But that Christ, and hys Apostles dyd neuer moue sedicion for temporall thynges, thou doest affirme it scantly. Ioiada. yea, and truly also, or elles shewe thou the contrary. Symon. In the. xv. chap. of the Actes, we do reade that Paule and Barnabas, had no small discencion, and reasonyng agaynst them, which dyd teache Circumsicion. Who wyll deny, circumcision to be an outwarde thyng? Ioiada. I vnderstande & call outward thynges,
that

that dooe helpe nothyng to our
saluacion, perteining to the bo=
dy, more, then to the soule, and
which being necessari to the bo=
dy, do, in processe of tyme, waxe
olde, waste, and consume away,
suche as be, condicion, rychesse,
and grosse elementes of thys
worlde. But circumcision, was
not taught by the false prophe=
tes, as an outwarde thyng, but
as a necessary & needefnl thyng
to saluacion: which thei dyd ve=
ry vrgently and instantly per=
suade, that it shoulde bee ob=
serued & kepte, yea, and all the
whole law besyde. Hereof, dyd
ryse the disputacion, whche is
written of, in the xb. chap. of the
Actes Els Paule dyd circum=
cise, Timothie, for peace and
tranquilitie sake, and because
that he woulde not offende certayne

tayne weake bretherne, in the
Churche: but after that, some
men dyd vrgently bring in, cir-
cumcison, as necessary, Paule
dyd greatly repugne, & woulde
not suffer Titus to be circumci-
zed. xvi. of the Actes. ii. Galat.
This sedicio͂ therfore that thou
aledgest here, hathe a greatter
cause, then an outwarde thyng.
 Sy. Howe darest thou call richesse outwarde thinges, which
do exclude a ma͂ from the kyngdome of Heauen ? For Christ
sayeth that it is easyer for a camell, to go thoroughe the eye of
a nydle. then for a ryche man to
entre into the kyngdome of Heuen. Io. We doo know well i-
noughe the false sighynges and
teares of the Crocodyle, which,
these light and inconstant Anababtistes, do poure doune daily,
                           dispisyng

Against the

dispisynge richesse, none other wyse, then the Foxe, dyd in tymes past dispyse, the sweete grapes, that she could not come by. Richesse, are by them selues nether good, nor euyll, but the vse, dothe make theim either good, or euyll. If thyne eye be simple, and lyghtsome, all the body shal be lyghtsome: but if thyne eye be wycked and euyll, all thy body shall be darkenesse. Mat. vi. Therfore, if a riche mā be faithfull and godly, the richesse that he hathe, be good, and that, by reason of the good vse. If the master or owner of the richesse, is vnfaythful or an infidell, his richesse are nought. Luke. xvi. Such, do christ speake of, when he bringeth in, the similitude of the camell. and of the eye of the nedle. There wer innumerable,

bothe

bothe in the olde & newe Testa=
ment, whiche, in great richesse
were called no small frendes of
God: as Noe, Abraham, Lot,
Isaac, Jacob. Job, Joseph, &c.
Whiche in the myddest of their
rychesse, dyd cleaue vnto God,
with a sincere harte, and good
fayth. Loke what opinió Paul
hathe of this thyng, and what
he writeth of it .i. Timoth. vi.
Therfore, I care not what these
hipocrites doo bable and prate,
sith that the richemen may doo
good to the poore, in Christes
Churche, whiche occasion they
that haue no richesse doo lacke.
To what purpose or intent doo
then these mad braines, trouble
all the worlde for trifelyng and
vnnecessary thyng(¿ I do know
sum, which, if thei had as much
as they do lacke, thorough their
owne

owne negligence and slugherd=
nesse, they woulde fynde by and
by a way, to iustify their vniust
and euyll gotten goodes. Sy.
I doo let that passe, I pray the,
to proue the seconde conclusion.
Peraduenture I shall learne
somewhat by it. Ioiada That
Christ dyd neuer cause tumult,
for outwarde thynges, but dyd
alwayes study to peace & tranquilitie, we wyl bring the .xvii.
of Mathew, where he speaketh
to Peter after this maner: Lest
we do offēd them (that is to say,
that do receyue the didragme)
go thy waye to the sea, & cast in,
thy hoke, and the fyrst fysh that
cometh, open his mouth, & thou
shalt fynde a stater, take it and
geue it for the & me. In the.xxii
of Math, when he was asked,
of the yearely tribute, that was
payed

the Anabaptistes.

payed vnto Ceasar, he did so fly from tumulte, that he dyd iyone bothe god and Ceasar togither, biddyng them to pay their duty to eche of them. Nor, he dyd not condempne them, that dyd receyue. Nor agayne he dyd not say: Blessed are they, which doo geue. He dyd not say: ye owe nothyng by Goddes law, but notwithstandyng geue: wo be, vnto hym, that dothe receyue. In the .xiii. of John, Christ doth so teache hys Disciples: I geue you a new cōmaundement, that ye loue eche other, as I haue loued you. By this, shall all men know that ye be my Disciples, if ye loue eche other. And incontinent in that long sermon that he made vnto his Disciples, after his Maundy, he doth chefely speake of the Spirite of the
faithfull.

faythfull. And a lytell afore, he
shoulde sende his Apostles, he
dyd saye: Peace vnto you, as
my father hathe sent me, so I
sende you. The.xiiii.chap.Rom.
Paule sayeth: The kyngdome
of God, is neyther meate nor
drinke, but rightousnesse, peace
and gladnesse in the holy ghost.
For, he that serueth vnto christ
in those thyngs, is accepted both
before GOD, and before men.
Therfore, let vs followe that,
whiche belongeth to peace, and
edifieng, one towarde another.
In the.i.Cor.i. he dothe exhorte
the Corinthiās, after this maner: I beseche you, brethren, in
the name of oure Lorde Ihesu
Christ, that ye dooe speake all
one thyng, and that there be no
dissenciōs among you, but that
yee bee one whole bodye, of one
mynde

mynde & opinion. Let no suche contenciōs be among you, that one shoulde say: I am Cephas disciple, another, I am Pauls: an other, I am Christes. Is Christ diuided: was Paul crucified for you? Or were ye baptised, in the name of Paule? When ye do say so, ar ye not yet carnal? Moreouer, loke, & consider what Paul writeth in the xii. cha. to the Cori. exhortyng them to concorde & charitie, by the exemple of the body and the lymmes. In the xiiii. he sayeth apartelye, that God is not aucthor of discencion, but of concorde and peace, whiche thyng may be sene, in the Churches of the faythfull. In the .iiii. to the Ephesians, Paule doeth exhort vs, to behaue oure selues, and walke so, as it doeth become the

vocacion

vocacion wherwith, we are called, with all obeisaunce & lowlynesse, with gentlenes of hert, forbearing eche other thorough charitie, and that we shoulde studye to kepe the vnitie of the spirite by the bounde of peace, beyng (sayth he) one body & one spirite, as yee are called in one hope, of your vocacion. There is but one Lorde, one fayth, one Baptisme, one God and father of vs all, &c. In the .ii. chap. to the Philippians, with lyke study, exhorteth he, the faythfull to be of lyke affection, to haue betwene them selfes, loue & charitie, to be of lyke mynde & lyke iudgement, and that nothyng shoulde be doone among them, by contencion or vayneglorye. But by humilitie & lowlynesse of hearte, euerye man shoulde thynke

thynke an other mā, to be more
excellent, then he is himself. &c.
Are not these, sufficient testi‑
monies? Sy. What dooe these
thynges agaynste the Anabap‑
tistes? Io. Very much, for thei
proue and shew manifestli, that
the Anabaptistes be authors of
tumulte and sedicion. Sy. What
is that? Ioi. That is to say, that
they against al good ordre, and
exemple of the Apostles, dooe
make stryfe & contencion in the
Churche of Christ, & that only
for certayne outwarde trifles.
Sy. But they doo teache many
thynges of God and of faythe.
What outewarde thynges are
they, wherfore they do make di‑
uision in the Churche? Ioi. If
they shoulde preache none other
thyng, but of God, of faith, cha‑
ritie and innocencye of lyfe, it
        I.iii.   shoulde

should be no neede of this seperacion. For these thynges are taught also in our Churches, so that it is no neede at all, that they shoulde preache. But they seperate them selues therefore, because that they teache these thynges hereafter rehersed, that is to saye: That we haue neede of a new Baptysme, and that a Christen man may not receyue rentes, nor reuenewes: That Christen men are free frome paiyng of tythes: That a christen man may not beare rule or be a maiestrate: That no man is boūde to make a lawful othe, when he is commaunded, by the maiestrates: And also they doo take away richesse from christē men. Are not these, outwarde thynges? And agayne, do they not for suche thynges diuide & trouble

trouble the Churche. Besyde that, they doo bynde their disciples, that they shall not heare the worde of God among them, where Baptysme of chyldren is vsed, rentes and tythes payed, any lawfull othe is made, magistrates be, & richesse ar counted good. Nowe call in remembraunce, the places and testimonyes, that we haue brought and aledged afore, of Christ, & of his Apostles, & ponder well, whether this seperation, is Apostolicall, or sedicious. Sy. It skylleth not that ye cal them sedicious. For that dyd chaunce to Christ, and to his Apostles, to be accused of tumulte & sedicion. But in this thyng, they do prayse God, and geue thankes, that they be counted worthy, to suffer for the name of Iesu, remem-

membring what Christ sayeth:
Blessed are ye when men dooe
curse you, and speake all euyll a
gainst you, reioice and be glad,
for your reward is great in heuen. Ioa. Why doest thou leaue
that clause which Christ added
vnto it, when he was speakyng
suche thynges? Sy. What haue
I lefte? Ioa. Lying (sayth he)
for my sake. That we dooe call
the Anabaptistes sedicious, it
is not doone for Christes sake,
but because, that they do diuide
Churches beyng well ordered
and pacified, for the thinges a-
fore named. The which thyng
neuer Christ nor his Apostles
dyd. Nor we doo not lye, when
we accuse them of tumulte, and
sedicion. For the thing is so manifest, that it can not be denyed.
But they that imputed suche
thynges

the Anabaptistes.

thinges to Christ, and to his Apostles dyd lye, and dyd not say trewe, as it appeareth by the xxiii. of Luke, the xvi. & xxiiii. of the Actes. There were some which dyd falsely reporte, that they preached agaynst paiyng of Tribute, vnto Ceasar, seducyng the comens, and mouyng sedicion, whiche thynges were not true. For neither christ, nor his Apostles dyd it, but rather taught the contrary alwayes. But the Anabaptistes, because, that they repugne against publike magistrates or rulers, and go aboute to abolysshe the ordinance of God, are ryghtfully called tumultuous, rebels and sedicious heretikes. Symon. I woulde gladly (if I myght obteyne that thyng of thee) that thou shuldest leaue, that word,

J.v. heretike,

Heretike: For as often as I heare it, I dooe all quake and tremble in my herte. Ioia. When I dooe say heretike, I dooe not vnderstande him, that the rude & vnlerned people doth meane, but him that is aucthor of sectes, and maketh diuision in the Churche, which doth obstinately breake and trouble the vnitie of the Churche, with false and erronious opinion. But I wyll bringe mo places to confirme my conclusion. Symon. I wyll gladly heare them. Ioia. In the xx. of the Actes. Paul speakyng vnto the ouerseers, beynge assembled togither, at Miletyng, dyd byd them to take heede to them self, & to the whole flocke, ouer the whiche, the holy gost hathe made them ouer seers, to gouerne the Churche of God, whiche

whiche he had purchased with his owne blood. For sayeth he, I do know this well, that greuous wolfes, shall after my departyng, entre in, not sparyng the flocke: euen from you shall ryse men, speakynge peruerse thynges, to drawe after them disciples. Thou seest, my Symon, the nature of heretikes, whiche is, to make diuision in the Churche, to get vnto them disciples, or folowers of their heresye, not to spare the flocke, to sowe discorde, to teache peruerse thynges, to allure men, to reyse or styr vp partes, sectes, & factions, to congregate a particuler Churche. Sy. These argumentes do almost touche the Anabaptistes. For they make diuision in the Churche, and do bring vp and maintayne a singularitie

gularitie amonge theim or by themselfes. But hast thou more testimonies or places? Ioiada Paule doth warne the Romaines with these wordes, saiyng: I pray you, brethren, that yee looke vpon them, that cause among you dissencion and strife, agaynste the doctrine that yee haue learned, & that ye do flye from theim. For they that are such, do not serue vnto our lord Iesu Christ, but to their belye, and by blandiloquence, & flatteryng, disceiue the hartes of the simple. Sy. This aucthoritie the Anabaptistes do vse, but agaynst you. Io. Consyder, my Symon, in your mynde, howe truly thei do bring such thyng? agaynst vs. Where dyd we euer make diuision in the Churche: whiche thynge is familier and proper

proper vnto them ? Where dyd we euer put offedicles, or stombling blockes, vnto the church? Where as, they haue made an innumerable sorte of mē so perplexed and doubtfull, that they do abhorre from the gospell & do beleue neither vs, nor them. Paule did more lyuely expresse them, that do disceyue & seduce the people with fayre speakyng, seruyng to their belyes, in the iii. chapiter to the Philipenses, with these wordes: For many do walke, of whom I haue spoken many tymes, and now doo speake weeping, enemyes of the crosse of Christ, whose ende is perdicion, whose belye is their God, and glorie or reioysyng, in their opprobriousnesse: Which do care for earthly thyngs only. Nowe iudge, my Symon, vnto whom

whom these thinges may be applied, vnto vs, or vnto the Anabaptistes. They vociferate and crye alwayes, agaynst Tythes, Tributes, Riches, Othes, Magistrates, propertie of goodes. We do preach Faith, Innocency of lyfe, Charitie, & that men may vse all thinges well, as the gyftes of God. Who boasteth more, or reioyseth in reprochefull thinges, then thei do, that is to say, in their Catabaptisme, or oppinion agaynst Baptisme, in forsakyng of their houhold, & in their slouthfulnes, wherin thei do wander aboute, as ydle vacaboundes. Moreouer, of these thynges, that they do teache, tumultes, sedicions, warres, robbyng and spoilyng, dyd alwayes ryse. I thynke thou doest vnderstande, whom Paule
dothe

do the call belyes, aud enemyes of the crosse of Christ. Sy. If thou hast any more testimonies or places, I pray you, hyde not them from me. Ioia. Touchyng the vnitie of the church against the Anabaptistes, ther is a singuler place, in the .x. of the Hebrues: Let vs (sayth he) consider, & looke one vpon another, for thys intent, that wee maye prouoke eche other to charitie, & good workes, not forsakyng the mutuall felowship or congregacion of vs, as some men ar wont to do. And what other thyng do the Anabaptistes, but for the weakenesse, or (as they doo say) for the wyckednesse or vngodlynesse, of some, forsake the Churche· and exhorte other to dooe the same. ⸝ But let vs come now to the .iiii. conclusion, which

which shall shew playnly, that the Anabaptistes are false prophetes, & enemyes of the Crosse of Christ. Sy. Bryng it furthe, that I may heare what it is. Ioia. They are false prophetes, whosoeuer they be, that doo affirme, that Christ dyd only abolish & take away, originall syn. They are false Prophetes, that do deny grace, & forgyuenesse of synnes vnto them: which, after that the truthe is once knowen, do fall agayne, into sinne or error. They are false Prophetes, that do attribute, saluaciõ, vnto our workes. Syth that the Anabaptistes do teach these articles, thei be not only enemies of the crosse of Christ, but more ouer do denye Christ. Sy. They do no suche thing. Iol. Though they do not with their mouthe.

denye

denye Chzist, yet notwithstandyng, thei do in very dede deny
the vertue, and strengthe of
Chzist, & of his death: as Peter
doth saye. ii. Peter. ii. forswea-
rynge the Lorde, that bought
them. Is not all one thyng, if
a man should say Chzist is not.
And there is no suche thynge,
wherefore Chzist dyd come?
Chzist dyd come to take away
our synnes, whiche thyng if he
dyd not, Chzist is not Chzist.
If he be dead onely for them,
that were in the old testament,
and not for vs, he can not bee
our sauiour, and how is he then
Chzist? If so be that our workes, do saue vs, is he not dead
in vayne? Doest thou not
see, how the enemyes
of the Crosse are
knowen?
              R.f.   The

Against

The .vii. Treatyse or Dialogue.

How that Christ dyd not onely suffer, for originall syn.

Symon.

Take hede, that thou doest not rashly and without aduisemēt, blame the Anabaptistes. For ther hath ben alwayes some, whiche dyd saye, that Christ hathe suffered onely, for them, that were afore him, that is to saye, for the Fathers, which dyd lyue vnder the olde Testament, & that he hath only pourged in vs, Originall synne, and that we ought to expiate, or to make amendes & satiffaction, with our owne dedes and workes, for the sinnes, that we cōmit, after that we be ones purified.

the Anabaptistes.

purified. Iol. If ye haue ben so taught hytherto, and haue beleued so, why was Peter Abelardus counted an heretike, & made to recant againe, by saint Bernarde, in the councell of Sens? He dyd teache very like thynges. Sy. This dothe moue me. but lytell. Ioiada. In this thinge, are yee blame worthye, that ye Anabaptistes, do know, neither new nor olde histories, & yet ye wyll be teachers. What audacitie is this? But howe vayne your opinion is, and how muche, it doth eneruate and asseablysh, the vertue of the passion of Christ, we wyll shew, by the holy scriptures. John Baptist, shewyng with his fynger, that pure & immaculate lambe Iesu Christ, dyd saye: This is the lambe of God, which taketh
away

awaye the synne of the worlde.
By these & other wordes of the
scrip.ure. it is manifestly proued, that Christ is the full satisfaction, for the synnes of all the
worlde. Or canst thou say, that
the fathers of the old Testamēt
are onely the worlde. Sym. No,
but he sayeth syn, & not synnes.
Ioi. John dothe vse this worde
synne, as he dothe, this diction
world. By the worlde, he vnderstandeth, whatsoeuer is world-
ly: so by this word sinne, he vnderstandeth, all that can be named synne, the gender beynge
here put, for the species. For he
sayeth, which taketh away, and
not, which hath taken away, or
shall take away, that this word
Tollit, taketh away, may signi-
fye action or doyng & not tyme.
For what synnes soeuer are taken

ken away, they ar taken away, by the sacrifice of Christ, done in the Crosse. Sym. Thou must bring cleare & more strong testimonies, for these, can easely be confuted. Ioia. This aucthoritie is bothe playne & strong inough. Nor it can not be subuerted, by any contradiction. But that thou mayest see, that we ar not without auctorities. Reade the .v. to the Roma. and thou shalt vnderstand, and perceyue, that the vertewe of the death of Christ, is abolyshed by you. And not as bi one mā (saith saynt Paul) which had sinned, death dyd come: so is the gyfte of GOD. For iudgement, dyd come, by one synne to condemnacion, and the gyfte dyd come, to iustify frō many synnes. Do not these woordes, O Symion, proove, that Chzist with hys death, dyd not clense oz pourge onely one synne, but all maner of synnes ⁊ But reade all the whole chapiter, and then, thou shalte vnderstande it better. Paule speaketh of Chzist in the ii. chap. to the Collossen. after this maner: And you (sayth he) when yee were dead thozoughe youre synnes oz in the przepucie oz vncircumcisiō of your flesh, he hath quykened also with him fozgyuyng vnto vs all our synnes. Because that in him dothe inhabite all plenitude oz perfection of God head cozpozally and ye are made perfect in him. Which thyng, truly, coulde not be, if he had not washed vs clene frō all our synnes. But the contrary is euidently knowen, by the .x. chap to the Hebzues. He

(sayth

(sayth saynt Paule) one oblacion beynge offered for synnes, sitteth euerlastigly on the right hande of God the Father. For with one oblaciō, he hath made perfecte for euer, them, that are sanctified. i. Joh. i. The blood of Christ, dothe clense vs, from all our synnes. i. Jo. ii. If any man dothe synne, we haue an aduocate, before the Father, that righteous Lorde Jesu Christ. And he is the satisfaction for oure synnes, and not onely for oure synnes, but for the synnes of all the worlde. If Christ dyd take away, onely original synne, the testimonye and aucthoritie of Jesu, is voyde. And agayne, if Christ dyed not for vs, but for them only that were after hym: what belongeth vnto vs, the death of Christ. Or why should we we confesse it, if it perteyneth nothyng vnto vs. Doest thou not see yet, who are false Prophetes, enemyes of the crosse of Christ, and subuersers of the Christen fayth. Sy. I doo see it well inough, and I am wel content, touchynge this Artikle. But as for that, that they dooe Denye, or wyll not graunt repentaunce, & grace vnto them, that befallen agayn: thei proue it strongly by the .vi. chap. to the Hebrues, and by the .ii. Peter. ii And, verely, as farre, as I can, perceyue, they speake well inough in it. That is to say, that we be no more in the flesh, and that we ought to synne no more after this: which thyng I wold thynke to be good, if we myght so pue. For they do so, very studiously & with great diligence.

the Anabbatistes.

The .viii. Treatye or Dialogue.

How that a synner may come to grace, as often as he repen=
teth, and that no man
is without synne.

Ioiada.

O Lorde God, that the sim=
ple, do so miserably suffer
themselues to be blynded.
If Menander & Symon, should
come agayne: I thynke they
coulde fynde adherentes, and
disciples, syth that the secte of
Nouatus & of the Catharians,
is so regarded & beleued among
many. Sy. What do these thinges
meane? Ioia That the seyd here=
tykes, dyd teache, about .xii. C.
yeares a go, the same thynges,
that thou hast nowe brought of
the Anabaptistes. For thei dyd

K b. Deny

Agaynst

deny all grace and forgeuenes, vnto them, that were fallen agayne: Thei dyd arrogate, and take vpon them, purenesse or clenlynesse of lyfe. They dyd congregate & assemble a particuler Churche, auoidyng and shunyng al cōmunion or felowship of synners. In the meane season, they dyd passe al mortal men, in presumptuousnesse and arrogancy, in enuy, hatered & contencion, in couetousnesse, & intemperancy of lyfe. But rede thou Cipzian, vpon the matter, in the .iiii. Epistle to Antonianus. The Anabaptistes if thou lookest better vpon the matter, are in all thinges lyke vnto the Catharians, and doo teache all one thyng with them. Suspecte them therefore. For he, that agreith, with manifest heretikes is lyuyng, condicions, conuer‍sacion & teachyng, can not teche the truthe, nor be a rightful mā. Or howe canst thou alow them whom all godly persones dyd alwayes abhorre? Sy. I care not for the Catharians, nor I know not, what the Cathariās be. That I do, in this thyng, a‍gree with the Anabaptistẻ, the scriptures compell me to do it, therfore I do not beleue them, but the scriptures. Ioia. This is that I haue sayde, and yet do I repete it, that nothing boldeth them so muche in their error as dothe ignoraunce. If they had read, and tasted the olde histo‍ries, thei wolde be more modest and sobre, and not so presump‍tuous. Is not this a miserable and perilous thyng, that men beyng so rude aud ignoraunt in all

Againſt

all thynges, do take vpon them, to be teachers. Wherby, it cometh to paſſe, that thei corrupt, confound & ſubuert al thynges, not hauynge the righte vnderſtādyng of ſcriptures. For that which Paule in the .vi. chap. to the Hebrues, and Peter in the ii. chap. of his ſecond Epiſt. doo write, dothe not ſtrengthe nor proue the oppinion of the Anababtiſtes, but that there is no remiſſion for them, whiche doo ſwarue frome the faythe, and thorow miſbeleue or infidelitie do diſpayre of the mercy of god. For they doo ſynne agaynſt the holy goſt, whiche ſyn is not forgyuen here, nor in the worlde to come, as Chriſte teacheth. Mat.xii. & .i. John. v. But, my Symon, diſcuſſe thou and wey, the wordes, of bothe the Apoſt-
tles,

stles, and consider to what purpose they were spoken. Truly for this purpose, to proue, that it is impossible for hym, that hath beleued ones perfectly, to falle away from his fayth. Peter, with the other disciples, being asked of christ, whether thei woulde, forsake hym also, dyd answere. Lord, to whom should we go? thou hast the wordes of euerlastyng lyfe. And we doo know and beleue, that thou art the sonne of the lyuyng God. If so be, that any man dothe fall cleane from fayth, he doth shew manifestly, that he had neuer a true fayth. They went from vs (sayth John) but they were not of vs: for if they had ben of vs, truly they shoulde had remayned with vs. He therfore, that swarueth from the knowē faith hathe

hathe no saluacion. But why?
For Christ is the onely saluaciō
frome whome he dooth falsely
swarue, and therfore can fynde
no other saluacion. Thou doest
vnderstande, I thynke, that the
falle, whereof Paull speaketh,
is not the fall, that doth chaūce
daily, by thinfirmitie & weakenesse of the flesh in them, that
are godly, but extreme desperacion thorough misbeleue & infidelitie, wherby a mā swarueth
from God. Reade the .vii. & .viii.
to the Heb. and thou shalte see,
that daily remission of synnes,
is not denyed vnto them that
ar fallen agayne. For he sayeth
also, in the .v. cha. that Christ is
a bisshoppe, that can haue com-
passion, of our infirmities, vnto
whom we must flye, hauyng ly-
cence & libertie, to do it. .x. chap.
to

the Anabaptistes.

to the Hebrues. Sy. In the .xii. chap. Paule teacheth . that Esau coulde fynde no place of repentaunce, thoughe he dyd seke it with teares. Ioia. Paule doth not speake in this place, of repentaunce, and forgyuenesse of synnes. but of election, and recouering of his first birth which he had lost ones, thorough glotony, and intemperance. and could neuer recouer it agayne, though he had assaied & proued it, with wepynges and teares. for Jacob had bought the right of the first borne, and had preuented him. Wherfore he speaketh nothyng heare, of the inwarde remission of sinnes. And often tymes, thys woorde penaunce is taken in an other significaciō. But the Cathariās dyd vse the same argumentes,
in so

in so muche, that some weake
persons, among them, that wer
godly. dyd abhorre, & suspecte
the Epistle to the Hebrues, as
some do now a dayes the Epi. of
saynt James. But now I come
to the auctoritie of Peter, who
speaketh after this maner: It
had ben better for them, not to
haue knowen the waye of righteousnesse, then after that they
haue knowen, to tourne from
that, that was taught them by
the holye precepte. But that
chaunceth vnto theim, that is
wont to be spoken in a true prouerbe: A dogge goynge to his
vomittyng (or to that which he
had vomitted) agayne: And a
washed sow, beyng retourned to
the myre wallowyng or walteryng. If thou consideresst well
& truly these wordes, thou shalt
fynde

fynde that they be spoken of infidelitie, and vnfaythfulnesse. From the which, after that thei wer ones called, through faith, they dyd fall agayn from God, into the fyrst vnfaythfulnesse & infidelitie. We doo see therfore that infidelitie is condempned euery where. Sy. What sayest thou of this, that thei do affirm that we liue no more in the flesh Io. The flesh dothe stycke vnto vs, to the verye graue. For the flesh doth contrary, the spirite, and agayne, the spirite doth repugne agaynste the flesh, in so moche that we doo that, whiche we woulde not do, the Rom. the vii. It is therfore great boldenesse, to presume & boast of that, whiche the Apostles dyd neuer presume ne boast of. For Paule did complain of his flesh, which
hath

hath more spirite, & dyd labour
more, to tame his flesh, then all
the Anabaptistes. And yet they
dare say, that they be not in the
flesh. For this cause peraduenture, because that they be, none
other thyng but flesh, that is to
say, all carnal, drouned in their
sensualitie & affections. Which
thyng is manifestly knowen, by
their lyfe. But paul did coclude
all thys whole matter, more
perfectly, & more briefly also,
saiyng: I do, with my mynde,
obey and serue vnto the lawe of
god, but with my flesh, vnto the
law of synne. He doth more, at
large expounde these thynges,
in the. viii. Rom. and v. Galat.
Where he dothe shewe, in fewe
wordes, that they, which do not
feare God, nor care, for heauenly thynges, but are all earthly,
do lyue after the flesh. And that

he walketh in the spirite, or after the spirite, which though he hath, & seeleth in him self, sinne, and weakenesse of the flesh, beyng tickeled with sensualitie, & affections, yet notwithstãdyng, dothe not geue the bridell, vnto the flesh, ne vnto synne, but resisteth styll, and is alwayes afrayde to fall. And if so be, that he chaunceth to fall, by and by, draweth he backe his foote, and repentyth. Sy, But they saye, that a man may be, without synloi. We are without synnes. as dogges be without fleas, in the moneth of August. O abhominacion, that men should thinke or presume suche thinges. I passe ouer here, that by this opinion, they doo blaspheme the veritie, of the gospel, yea, & take vtterly away the grace & mercy of God

L.ii. For

For where synne is not, there is no grace, where preuarication and transgression is not, there is no Remission amonge them, there is no transgression, ergo, the grace of God, is not among them. Is not this, to abolish the grace of God? What shall I saye, but that these mad braynes, do fal into another heresye, that is to saye, into the heresy, of that blasphemous mā Pelagius, who dyd denye the grace of God, magnifiyng and extollyng the strengthe of man. He was .xi. C. yeares ago. Sy. But they proue thys, with scriptures. Ioia. The veritie of the scriptures dothe teache nothing so. Beside that, thou canst bring no exemple, but the exemple of Lucifer, which woulde be lyke vnto God, as they wyll be without

without synne, wheras no man can be pure, and without synne, but God onely. Sy. Dothe not John say, that he, whiche is of God, synneth not? Ioia. He synneth not to death. Sy. Thou doest so expoūd it, or this is thyne exposicion. Ioai. Consider the wordes that go afore, and thou shalte vnderstand, that I saye true. Sy, What synne is that? or is not a man without synne, when he synneth not to death? Io. Christ saieth vnto the Iues: If ye do not beleue, ye shal dye, in your synnes, Ergo, vnfaythfulnesse is a deadly synne or syn to death. And though a faythful beleuer, is without this syn, that is to say, without infidelitie, yet he is not without vyce or syckenesse, which he must beware of always, lest he be drouned

ned in syn, or soiled & defiled w̄
the abhominable fylthynesse of
sinnes: & therfore it followeth
in John: We do know, that all
that is borne of god, sineth not:
but he that is borne of god, doth
kepe himself, & the euyll toucheth
him not. So therfore the godly
sineth not: & though he falleth
by frailnes, yet notwithstādinge
that malicious Satan can not
catche him. For the diligent study & labor, that the godly dothe
take, in shunnynge & auoidyng
synne (that is to say faith) doth
that syn is not imputed for syn.
It is written in the. viii. Rom.
That ther is no condemnacion
vnto thē that be in christ, which
do not walke after the flesh, but
after the spirit. Els saint John
doth say in the same self epistle:
If we do say, we haue no syn, we
deceyue our selfs, & truth is not

in vs. If we do cófesse our sines
god is both faithful & rightwise
to forgeue vs our sinnes, and to
clense vs from our iniquitie. If
we do say, we haue no synne, we
make him a lier, & his worde, is
not in vs. There be many suche
places euery where in the scriptures. Dauid doth crye out: O
Lorde, do not enter into iudgement, with thy seruaunt, for in
thi sight, no ma shalbe iustified.
And agayne, if thou lookest ex-
tremely vpon our synnes, o lord
who is able to abyde it & In the
xliii. of Esa. the lord doth speke
thus, by the Prophet, vnto the
Jues, which dyd glorify & boast
them selues in the rightwysnes
of ý law. I am he, I am he (saith
ý lord) that taketh away thyne
iniquities, for myne owne sake,
& wyll not remembre thy sines.
L.iiii.   Bring

Bring me into remembraunce, let us be iudged together, telle furth if thou hast any thyng, to iustifie thy selfe. Thy father hath synned fyrst, and thyne interpreters haue gone out of the way. None of the most holy men were euer without sinne, which thyng manifestly appereth, in Adam, Noe, Abraham, Isaac, Jacob, Moyses, Aaron, Dauid Josias, Ezechias, Peter, Paul, Matew. &c. Therfore Job speaketh truly. Job. ix. What am I, that I should answer him, and speake with him, with my wordes, which though I had some rightwysnesse, wyl not answer, but entreate my iudge. If I wyll iustifye my selfe, my mouth shall condemne me: if I say that I am innocent, my mouth shall proue me wicked. &c. Paule in
the

the.iii. Rom. sayeth, that al men haue sined, & do want the glory of god. In þ.xiii. of Jhon, christ sayeth, he that is washed hath no neade, but to wash his feete: for he is all cleane. If he be all cleane, what neade bathe he, to wash his feete? If he hath neade to wash his feete, how can he be all cleane? Therfore we ar clensed & purified, with the blood of Christ, that was shed vpon the crosse, from the filthines of syn, & be all cleane, But it followeth not by this, that we be no more i the flesh, or that we be no more synners. For the dregges of syn do remayne in our feete, that is to say, in our attections, as long as we liue, & walke in this dusti and foule way, we are soyled & contaminated, with the filthynesse of synne, which we neade,

with

with perpetuall study and daily care, to washe awaie, and afterwardes, to wype out, these filthinesses, with gret inward grefe repentaunce, and teares, in the vertue of the passion and death of Chryst. Finally chrift, in the .xv. of John saieth: I am the trewe vine, and my father is the husbande man. He doeth take awaie every bough in me that bringeth forth no fruite, & every bowgh ÿ bryngeth forthe fruite, he doeth purge & make cleane, that he mai bryng forth more fruite. By the which saiynges we maie vnderstande, ÿ we that are in Christ, thorowe faith, as a bowgh, is in ÿ vine, & doo bryng forth fruite, liuyng godly, haue neuerthelesse nede to be made cleane, and that, by the spirit, and vertue of Christ.

Now,

the Anababtistes.

Now, ẏ, which is made cleane, must nedes to be vnpure, & vn=clene. So we, that ar in Christ alredy ar made clene daily, for we do offend in many thinges, and no man is liuyng, that sin=neth not, and that hath no nede of this clensyng. Except the A=nababtistes, whiche in their bathe, be made so pure & clene, by their water, wherwith thei do wash their disciples, among whom, water doeth take awaie that, which the blood of Christ doeth not take awaie in them, that are godly. Sy. I do not see yet proued, that he, which fal=leth againe, after that he hath knowen the truthe, doeth daily fynd grace & pardon. Io. It is sufficientli proued by ẏ saiyngs of Iohn, and by the exemple of Dauyd, and of Peter. For if
we be

we be all synners, and yet neuerthelesse doo entre, into the kyngdome of heauen, where no vncleane thing entreth, it foloweth that our synnes are forgyuen vs. Sy. I do not denay, but that we were ones all synners, & that those synnes were ones forgyuen vs, by Chryste. But I will saie this, that after that the synnes, which we committed before, thorow ignorãcye, be ones, thorow the grace of God forgyuen vs, and so bee receaued by the free gyfte and goodnesse of Chryst, in to ÿ numbre of the chyldren of god, that then we be pure holy, and clene, and that we ought to synne no more, and that, if we synne wittyngly, after that we haue ones knowen & receaued the grace, such sinne is not forgiuen. Io.

the Anababtistes.

But thou mightest, sufficiently vnderstand by the places afore aledged, that we be yet sinners styll, after that we haue knowen the truthe, and that those sinnes, which we do daily commit as long, as we ar in Christ be daily forgyuen vnto vs. For Chryste saieth, that his disciples, are all cleane, but neuertheleffe that thei haue neade to wasshe their fete. And again, the father dooeth make cleane the bowghes, that doo bring forth fruite in Christe. If thei dooe bryng forth fruit, thei do bring forth fruite, in faith, and in the knowen truthe (for without faith, it is impossible, that any man shulde please God, & what so euer is without faith, is sine and not fruit.) If thei be made cleane, thei haue some filthines

in

in the knowen truthe. Els thei
shulde be cleane, and shuld nede
no clensynge or purgynge. But
sith that thei be made clene, the
filthinesses that thei do gather
in bringyng forth fruit, ar forgeuen and washed awaie. Neither Pelagius, nor Nouatus,
nor none of the Anabaptistes,
is able to withstand this veritee. Sy. I am not farre frome
this opinion, yet notwithstanding, had I euer to heare plain
scriptures, that a man, maie
come to grace, as often, as he
synneth. Io. And that can I
shew vnto the, besyde, the fore
aleged places. The lorde speaketh thus by Ezechiell: Wheu
the vngodly shall turne from þ
vngodlines, that he hath done,
& doeth iudgement & rightwisnesse, he shall get life vnto his
soule

soule. Is the death of ȳ vngodly, a pleasure vnto me, saieth ȳ lorde, and not rather, that he turne from his waies and liue? Turne and repent from al your iniquitees, and your iniquitee shall not hurt you. In the. ii. of Ioel. Turne to ȳ lord your god (saieth he) for he is gentill, and piteful, he is pacient, & of great mercifulnes, & repenteth vpon ȳ plage, ȳ he had threatened. Sy That, whiche thou hast aleged, is to be vnderstanded of the vngodly, & of ȳ remission of sinnes ȳ is graunted vnto them, that neuer knew god, & neuer beleued in him. Io. I wold ȳ thou shuldest loke better vpon ȳ wordes of Ezechiell, thou shuldestse, ȳ he speaketh these woordes to ȳ children of Israell, whiche were the chosen people of god.

Mose-

Agaynst

Moreouer considre, with what ende, he dooeth conclude this chapiter. Why shoulde ye dye (saieth he) o ye house of Israel, I wyll not the death of a sinner but ẏ hereturn & lyue. Or canst thou returne to hym, with whõ thou wast neuer before? Sy. No, but I doo come to hym, and do not returne, but with whom I was afore, and from whome I was gone, to hym doo I return againe. Ioi. Ergo it foloweth, that they, which are exhorted, by the prophete, to returne to god, were somtymes with god. If thei were sometymes with god: ergo this is not the fyrste sinne, that thei did committe, afore that thei knew the truthe but it was the synne, that thei committed, after that thei knew the truthe and had faith.

We

the Anabaptistes.

We haue proued, I thynke, that the synnes that we comit after the knowledge of the truth, are forgeuen, by God. In the xxiiii of the Prouerbes, it is written that a rightwyse man falleth vii. tymes in the day, & ryseth agayne, but that the vngodly do fall, to their vtter dampnacion. Here thou hast a manifest and a playne difference, betwexte the godly & the vngodly, or betwixt the faithfull & infidell. The vngodly, after that he is come, into the bothomlesse pitte, of vngodlynesse, dothe contempne, & remayneth in synne to the last ende with dispayre. A godlye man, is not he that synneth not, but he, which falling. vii. tymes in the day, doth not continew in synne, but ryseth agayne. With this place, are the Palagians,

Agaynst

Nouatians, and Anabaptistes confounded & conuicted. Adde vnto these the .xviii. of Mat. & the .xvii. of Luke, where Christ doth plainly say: If thy brother do the trespasse agaynst the, rebuke him betwixte the and him alone, if he be sory for his offence or repenteth, forgeue thou him. And if he .vii. tymes in the day do the offende the, & .vii. tymes in the day cometh to the saiyng: I am sory for myne offéce, thou shalt forgeue him. Sy. But he doth not saye, that he wyll forgeue vs our synnes. Ioia. Canst thou pray, or say thy Pater noster? Sy. yeas. Ioia. Doest thou not thou pray this: Forgeue vs our trespasses, as wee forgeue them that trespasse against vs? Unto these woordes dothe the Lord adde, by and by, in the. vi.

chapiter

chapiter of Mathew. If ye doo forgeue vnto men their fautes your father, that is in heauen, shall forgeue you also. Seyng therfore, that wee doo forgeue, vnto oure brethren daily, it foloweth, that the father of heauē forgeueth vs also daily. Do not the saintes or holymen pray so, and that euery day? Nowe, I aske the, whether they do lye before God: praiyng thus or uot? S. They do not lye. Io. If they do not lye, it foloweth, that thei haue in them selfe trespasse and synnes. If so be, that synne, as thou thynkest, is not forgeuen, whye dyd Christe teache vs to prai so: forgeue vs our trespas. Is not this an abhominable thyng, that any man, whiche knoweth not, what he dooeth praye, shoulde take vpon hym,

not

not only to be a teacher, but also to teache that whiche repugneth against ẏ manifest truth and prayers of the Sayntes⸫ But what thynkest thou of Peter, was he, a faithfull Christen man, & elected of God, or not⸫ Sy. He was not a faithful Christen man, afore his falle, els he wolde not haue denyed Christ. Ioi. If he had ben an infidel, to what intent were these wordes spokē. mat.xvi. Thou art christ the son of the lyuyng god⸫ Are these the wordes of an infidell. And agayne, if Peter had ben, an infidell or hipocrite, when he dyd make suche a godly confession, Christ would not haue sayde: Thou art blessed Symō: flesh and blood hath not reuelated this thynge, vnto the, but my father, which is in heauen.
The

the Anabaptistes.

The LORDE prayseth not, hipocrites and infidels, but abhorret & hateth them, Mat. vi and .xxiii. He would not haue said vnto him: he that is washed, hath no neade, but to washe his feete. And agayne, Peter, I haue prayed for thee, that thy faith do not faile or slake. Rede besyde that, the .xvii. of Iohan. Now I aske the again, whether Peter was a faythful Christen mam, or not? Sy. The scripture doth compel me to confesse, that he was a faithfull christē man. Io. Now I aske agayn, whether his fall, was a synne or not? Sy. Agayne, the scripture cōpelleth me, to confesse that it was a synne, for he dyd wepe bitterly And agayn, if to deny christ, is no synne, what shalbe a syn thā Io. Ergo, it followeth, by all

M iii. these

these argumentes, that Peter dyd synne, after the knowledge of the truthe, and receiuyng of the fayth. Therfore, a faythfull man is not all without synne. And here Peter dyd committe not a small, but a very greuous synne, denyeng thus, the Sauior of the worlde. Now I aske whether his synne was forgeuē him or not? Sy. yeas truly: for Christ sayeth: Whan thou arte turned agayne, conforte or confirme thy brethren. Ioia. So shoulde the Anababtistes dooe, if they were sent by God. But seeyng that presumptuousnesse & partinacie hath sente them, and do so bytterly, & with suche stubburnesse, speake agaynst the gospell, teachyng for conforte, desperacion: they ar such Prophetes, as the Lorde doth complayne

the Anababtistes.

playne vpon, in Ezechiel, which regarde nor care nothynge for the diseased & wounded sheepe, (which thing neuerthelesse, thei had learned of the Lord, which is deseruingly called the good & true shephearde. Luc.xv. or of Paule.ii. Corin.ii.) but dissipate & scatter the Lordes flocke. For what maketh them, besyde a singularitie, or singuler loue of them selfes, to separate them selfes, from our church, but that (as they do say) we be synners, that is to say, vsurers, publicās & dronkardes? I can not, but that I must cōfesse, that ther be many enorme sines vsed amōge vs (which is the more pitie) yet we ought not to dispayre of many, but that thei mai be brought to repentaunce. And truly, as for our selues, we are not very

M.iiii. negli=

negligent or slouthfull in rebu-
kynge synnes, cryinge out styll
bitterly agaynst them, that com-
myt suche thynges. And yet a-
gaynst the precepte of GOD,
Math. xiii. and exemple of the
Apostles, which dyd condemne
no man rashly, they do separate
them selues from vs. But this
is the nature of Phariseis. Sy.
As touchyng this article, I am
sufficiently taught, & I thanke
God of it, Iaia. John, without
exception, doth say: Chyldren,
I haue written this vnto you,
that ye shulde not synne, but if
any man dothe synne, we haue
our aduocate, before the father,
that rightwise LORDE Iesu
Christ. &c. Here no man can
bryng any cauillacion. Christ
is here named and appoynted
to be Aduocate or mediator for
all

the Anabaptistes.

all synners, and that, at all ty=
mes, as he offereth him selfe.
ri. Mathew, saiyng: Come vn=
to me all ye that labor and are
loadyd, aud I wyll refresh you.
That same thyng doeth Paule
teache, concernynge the onely
Sauior Jesu Christ .i. Tim. i.
It is a faythfull saiyng, and
worthi to be receiued of al men,
that Christ dyd come, into this
worlde to saue synners. If the
Anababtistes therefore, dooe
teache the contrarye, they are
the open enemyes of the Crosse
of Christ: in the which opinion,
if they doo abyde, or persist ob=
stinately, they are manifest he=
retikes, whome all godly
persones ought to
flye and ab=
horre.

M.v.   The

The. ix. treatie or dialoge.

How that our saluacion and rightwisnesse, is not to be descrybed to our workes but to faith.

Symon.

If the Anababtistes doo teache, that our saluacion, & rightwisnes, ought to be ascribed to our workes (whiche is the. iii. parte of this article) thou wilt not saie (I thynke) that thei doo erre in it. Iosida. There is nothyng that I will graunt them. lesse. For this thynge beynge ones graunted, al y epistles of Paul ar condemned, as false, & whiche dyd seduce the people. For this is the thyng onely, wherfore Paule, with suche a zeale did repugn & resist against false prophetes, whiche did teache, that

that rightwisnesse dyd come of workes: where as sainte Paul did attribute our rightwisnes to faithe. That maie easily bee sene by ẏ epi. to the Ro. and to the Gala. But I wil bring out of them, certaine places, which can not be confuted. In the .iii. cha. to the Romains, Paul saieth thus: All haue synned and ar destitute of the glory of god but are iustified freely by his grace, thorowgh the redemcion that is in Christ Iesu. And in the .iiii. Ro. If Abraham were iustified by workes, thē hath he wherin to reioice, but not with god, for what saieth ẏ scripture Abrahā beleued god, & it was counted vnto him, for rightwisnes. To him ẏ worketh is ẏ rewarde not reckened of fauoure but of dutye. To him ẏ worketh

not

not, but beleueth in hym, that
iustifieth, the vngodly, is his
faith counted for rightwisnes.
Euen as Dauid describeth the
blessedfulnes of that man, vnto
whom god imputeth righwis-
nesse without dedes. Blessed ar
thei (saieth he) whose iniquities are forgiuen, & whose sinnes are couered. &c. And in the
xi. to the. Ro. There is a reme-
naunt left accordyng to the e-
lection of grace, if it be of grace
then it is not now, of workes.
For thã grace is no more grace
But if it be of workes, then is
it no more grace. For then wer
deseruyng, no more deseruyng.
In the seconde to the Galathians: The lyfe, whiche I nowe
lyue in the fleshe, I lyue by the
faith, of the sonne of God, whiche loued me, and gaue hym
self

selfe for me, I despise not the grace of God. For if rightwisenesse cometh of the lawe, then Chryste, is dead in vaine. In the thyrde chapiter, he doeth argumente and reasone after this maner: That no man is iustified in the sight of God, by the lawe, it is euydent. For the iuste shall lyue by faythe. The lawe is not of faythe, but the man, that fulfylleth the thynges, conteyned in the law, shall lyue in them. Chryst hath delyuered vs from the curse of the lawe, in as muche, as he was made accursed for vs, that the blessing of Abraham might come on the gentilles thorough Ihesu Chryste, and that we myght receaue the promise of ÿ spirit, thorow faith. Brethern, I speake after ÿ maner of men.

Thowgh

Though it be, but a mans testament, yet if it be alowed, no man despiseth it, or addeth any thyng thervnto. To Abraham, and his sede, was the promise made. He saieth not, in thy sedes, as in many, but in thy sede as of one, which is Christ, this I saie, that the lawe, which beganne. CCCC and .xxx. yeres after, doeth not disanulle the testament, which was confirmed afore of God, vnto Christwarde, to make ỹ promise of no effecte. For if the inheritaunce cometh of ỹ law, then it cometh not of ỹ promise. But god gaue it, vnto Abraham by promise. For if ther had ben a law geuē, which could had geuen life, thē no doubt rightwisnesse, shoulde haue comed by ỹ lawe. But the scripture, concluded al thinges

vnder sinne, ẏ the promise, by ẏ
faith of Jesu Christ, might bee
geuen vnto them ẏ beleue. In ẏ
ii.cha. to the Ephe. ye ar saued
thorow faith, & not of our owne
selues. It is the gift of god, and
cometh not of our dedes or workes. For we ar his owne worke-
mashyp, created in Jesu Christ
to do good dedes, which he hath
prepared for vs to walke in, &
in the.iii.to Ti.we wer also fo-
lyshe, disobediente, deceaued,
seruyng to lustes and voluptu-
ousnes, liuyng in malice, and
enuye, hatefull or odiouse and
hatyng eche other. But after ẏ
the goodnes and loue of our sauiour God, not accordynge to
the dedes of rightwisnes, whiche we haue done, but accordyng to his mercye, had made
vs safe, by the fountayne of
rege-

regeneracion, and renuynge of the holy ghost, whiche he hath poured vpon vs abundantely, thorow our sauiour Jesu christ that we beyng iustified by his grace, shulde be made heyres of euerlastyng lyfe, accordyng to our hope. These places are plaine, and can not be auoided. For thei, that speake againste them, are no christen men, but felowes of the false Apostles, against whome Paule writeth, callyng them euyll workemen, and subuersours of the gospell of Christ. And by these wordes, not onely the Anababtistes, but also, all popishe doctours, are noted, and whoso euer besyde, doo attribute our rightwisnes and saluacion to our dedes & workes. Sy. I can saie nothing against the manifest veritee.

But

the Anabaptistes.

But I wold faine know of the, in what reputacion thou haste the epistle of Iames, and how muche thou doest esteme it. Io. And I aske the first, what thou thinkest, oz what oppinion and iudgement thou haste, of the afoze aledged places, and howe strong thou coutest them to be. Sy. Thei are manifest, and true and also strong enoughe, and dooe attribute saluacion, and iustifiyng: to faith, but Iamis doeth adscribe saluacion to our woozkes and dedes. Ioiada. What semeth vnto the then — is it right, ỹ many places, shulde geue the ouer hande to one, oz one place to many. Symon. The interpzetació of one place, must bee taken out of many. But what dooeth this to the epistle of Iames? Ioiada. Had the apostles

apostles all one learnynge and
spirite ⸗ Symon. All one. But I
asked the, touchynge the wor﹀
des of James. Ioiada. I haue
had alwaies in singulare repu﹀
tacion, the epistle of James,
and haue alwaies geuen great
credit & a faith vnto it, though
it hath ben suspected by Euse﹀
bius, and other besyde, & coun﹀
ted lesse apostolicall. But if it
be Apostolical, it foloweth, that
it hath the same meanyng and
spirit, that the epistles of Paul
haue. For this thou hast graū﹀
ted before, that thei had al one
learnyng and spirit, moreouer
that the places, whiche I haue
aledged out of Paule, and doo
adscribe saluacion to faythe,
and not to woorkes, are bothe
true and stronge. Now it folo﹀
weth necessarily that it is not
the

the meanynge of James, that wooxkes shoulde iustifye and saue, and that therefore this darke place and saiyng of James ought to be expounded, by many plaine and manifeste testymonyes of Paule. Symon. What is that? Ioiada. That is to saie, that James dooeth not goe about, to proue, that workes iustifie, and that fayth iustifieth not, but that faithe without workes, is no faithe, but an oppinion and credulitie, or light beleue, which faith can not saue. And y it is sufficient to saluacion to trust & leyne vpon this vaine oppinion. It is manifest therfore, y James doeth not take here faith, for that true and liuely faithe (whiche faith is a gyft of God, and renuyng of the mynde, and lyfe) but

but for a false oppinion, which foolysshe men do call faith, with the whyche faythe, the diuell beleueth, all quakyng and tremblyng, but by it, he is made neuer the better, nor saued. Besyde that, he vnderstandeth not humaine or bare workes without faithe, but faithe workyng effectually thorough charitee and loue. Ponder the wordes of saynt James, and thou shalt perceiue, that he proueth there, partly, that faithe can not bee without workes, partly that faith workyng thorough charitee, doeth bothe iustifie and saue. Therefore James dooeth not disagree from Paule, but meaneth al one thing with him agreyng, both in one spirit and learnyng. Sy. Yet it semeth vnto me, that our saluacion is adscribed

scribed to workes, when it is attributed to faythe. For if faith can not be without workes, nor workes without faith, thei must be all one thyng, and that, which is attributed to one is attributed to the other. Ioia, faith and workes are almost so one thynge, as the godhed, and manhead, are one persone in Christe. And yet it folowed not that the godhed is mortal, because that Christ dyed in very dede vpon the crosse. Yet not withstandyng, it is all one persone. whyche can not be diuided. So we maie speake in this busynesse. Faith iustifieth. Here faith is taken, for the election, and grace of God, and also for the redempcion, whiche is not adscribed to our owne workes, though thei can not be separated

ted from faith, and which folowyng most certainly of faithe, are very sure & vndoubted signes & tokens of faith and election of god. For so Paul doeth speake: Whom he hath predestinated them dydde he chose, whom he hath chosen, them did he call, whome he hath called, them dyd he iustify. And John also: We knowe, that when he shall appere, we shall bee lyke vnto hym, and euery man that hath this hope, doth make him selfe cleane, as he is pure. i. Jo. iii. In one sonne, there is both lyght and heate, and the one is not from the other. Yet notwithstandyng the lightyng or illuminacion, is attributed to the lyght, and not to the heate, and the heatyng or warmenesse, is adscribed to the heate, and not to

the Anabaptistes.

to the lyght. Symon. But the scriptures dooe often and in many places, abscribe saluacion, to oure woorkes and merites. Ioiada. That is done, not because that the worke, shoulde bee barely taken by it selfe, but as a woorke or dede, compyng of faithe, wherby that, whiche is farthest, and chyefest (that is to saie faythe) maie be manifested, and shewed. I aske the, can a man, dooe any good thynge of hym selfe. Symon. No. For no man, is good, but god onely. Ioiada. And Christ saieth in the. xb. of Iohn. As boughes can not brynge forthe fruite, excepte, they remayne stylle, in the vine. So ye can bryng forthe no fruite excepte ye remayne in me. For without me, ye can dooe nothynge.

N.iiii. Now

Againſt

Now I aſke againe, who bringeth forth the grapes and the wyne? Symon. The vine. Ioia. If god, ſhoulde take awaie his ſtrengthe frome the vyne, and ſhoulde not worke in it, that, which we dooe ſee, coulde that vine bryngeforthe wyne? Sy. No. Ioiada. The chyefe thyng therefore that geueth wyne, is not the vyne, but God, and yet notwithſtandyng, we dooe adſcribe the wyne to the vyne, where as it dooeth onely come of God. Symon. I can ſaye nothynge agaynſte the truthe. Ioiada. It is all one reaſon, when the ſaluacion and euerlaſtynge lyfe, is attributed to oure owne workes, where as it cometh of God onely, and of gratuitee and free election. For GVD worketh in vs,

bothe

the Anababtistes.

bothe to be willyng, and to doo or performe the thyng, that he hathe moued vs, to be willyng to do, accordyng to his bountnous wyll. He, I say, worketh in vs good workes, as in his electes, notwithstanding the workes ar attributed vnto vs, and are called ours, whiche neuerthelesse are Gods, that glory & honor may be geuē to god only. Doest thou vnderstande what I say? Sy. I doo vnderstand it very well. Ioia. Dothe it satisfie thee? Sy. yeas truly, Now do I perceiue, that the lernyng of the Anababtistes, cometh of ygnoraunce and boldnesse, and that it is very pernicious and hurtfull, whiche is gaye in the syght of the simple, but in dede is an error, & malicious rudenesse. But I desyre to knowe,

N.v.   what

Against.

what thou wylte saye of the .v. conclusiō: For they be fully persuaded, that soules are a slepe.

The .x. treatie or dialoge.

How that the Soules after that thei be departed from the body do not slepe, but lyue in christ.

Ioiada.

But, with this opinion, they do abolish the gospel, which teacheth of the resurrection of Christ: as saynt Paule, in the fyrst chap. to the Romayns, doth say: Besyde that, they doo denye, the last Article of oure fayth, that is to saye: The lyfe euerlastyng, after this lyfe. Is not this therfore a pernitious Doctrine, that repugneth agaynst so manifest veritie, and sure beleue? Sy. Thou doest not vnderstande the Anababtistes,

for

For they doo neyther denye the Gospell, nor the Resurrection of Christ. They saye that the Soules, after the deathe of the bodye, (if they dooe departe in fayth) do slepe in the bosome of Abraham, tyl the day of iudgement, & that then, they do entre into euerlasting life. And proue their saiynges by the gospell, & by Paule. Luc.xvi. i.Thess.iiii. I wyl not haue you to be ignoraunt touchyng them, that are aslepe. &c. In the Olde Testament, it is written of the Fathers, that thei fal aslepe, with their Fathers. And also, it is sayde of Stephen, that he dyd slepe in the Lord. And that ther at lengthe, shall receyue euerlastyng lyfe, they do proue it by Paule .ii. Timoth.iiii. I haue sayeth he, fought a goodfyght. Now

Now is there layde vp for me, a croune of rightwysnesse, which the Lorde, who is a rightfull iudge, shall geue or render vnto me, vpon that day, not onely to me, but also to al them that loue his comynge. There is suche a thyng. Phil. iii. & .i. John. iii. Or what neade is it, of that last iudgement, if by & by, after his death, euery man receyueth his owne dome: these do seme vnto me strong. Nowe wyll I fayne heare what thou canst saye agaynst it. Io. I saye the same thyng that I sayde before. If our soules dooe sleepe, after the death of the bodye, the soule of Christ sleepeth also, and the resurrection is disanulled. For Christ dyd proue that ther was an euerlasting lyfe by his rising agayne, which can not be euerlastyng

lastyng, if the soule slepeth, and
begynneth then to lyue, when
iudgement dothe come. Wherfore
the sleepe of the Anababtistes,
dothe euacuate and disanull,
the gospell and resurrection.
As for the bosome of Abraham,
I aske the whether it
be, a slepyng place & dormitori,
or a receptacle, and place to receyue
the lyuyng? Sy, A place
wher vnto, the soules of y[e] faithfull
Christen men, ar gathered
to gether, tyll the day of iudgement.
Ioi. Where is that place,
aboue, or benethe? Sy, It is vncerteyne
to me, God doth know.
Nor it is not lawfull for vs, to
enquyre Sy. So ye do defend al
vncertayne thynges, that ye do
teache. And ye that do speake &
babble muche of the bosome of
Abraham, and do not know yet
what

what it is. The bosome of A-
braham, is the sosietie and felowship, of all them, whiche in
the olde testament, dyd departe
out of this worlde, in the fayth
of Abraham, which faithe was
in christ to come. For thei were
all saued by Christ. Nowe J
aske the whether they were not
all, by Christ Jesu, brought in
to the euerlastyng felicitie and
ioy. Sy. Dydest thou not vnderstande before, that the soules of
all the godly, do slepe in the bosome of Abraham, & are kepte
to the iudgement. Iol. These
sayenges are to abhominable,
my Symon, & to blasphemous
agaynst the gospel of Christ, to
say, that they, which were in the
bosome of Abraham, ar not yet
deliuered & broughte into heauen. What other thynges is it
els

els, but to saye, that heauen is not yet opened by Chzist. How muche dothe this doctrine, repugne agaynst the woozdes of Chzist. John, xiiii. In my fathers house ther be many mansions, if it were otherwyse, I wolde haue sayd vnto you, I go to pzepare yon a place. And if I go (that is to say, by my death) to pzepare you a place, I wyll come agayne, & take you, to my selfe, that where I am, there ye may be with me. Tell me, Simõ where is chzist, in the bosome of Abzahã, oz wher. S. In heauen on þ right hand of god þ father. I. Very wel: therfoze we shalbe also, in heuen, & not in the dozmitozy of Abzaham. Sy. But it shalbe then, whẽ Chzist cometh agayne. Foz he sayeth: I wyll come agayne, & take you to me.

That

Agaynst

That comyng of Chaist shall be in the last day of all. Ioia. What and I vnderstande that, of the comyng of Christ, at the ende of euery mans lyfe ⸭ Sy. So thou doest say: but it must be proued by the holy scriptures. Io. These ar not my wordes, but the wordes of him, that speaketh there, of his owne death. For he vseth this word, to go, for to dye. (So that to go, and to dye, is all one thyng, with him) And agayne, this worde, to come, wherfore the Anababtistes doo stryue, is not taken, for his last comyng, but for the resurrectiō of christ: and ye helpe and ayde, that he sheweth vpon the faythfull christen men being in extreme nede. For he came agayne, after that he was rysen from death, ⁊ dyd declare, that he had opened the

kyng=

kingdom of god: that we might be sure, that as he dyd entre in to heauen him selfe, so we shuld come in or entre in also. But he is entered, in to immortal lyfe, & not in to slepe, in to the kyngdome of God, and not in to the bosome of Abraham, and that by & by after his death. Therfore we shall also, incontinent after our death, entre in to euerlastyng lyfe, and into the kingdome of God. For he taketh vs away, when he calleth vs from death to lyfe. John.v. For it is added by maner of exposicion: That where I am, ther ye may be also. Therfore are we taken in soule, from death to euerlastyng lyfe, & in body, to iudgement. Or tell me, dyd Christ with his death, reserate & open heauen, whiche was locked vp afore

afore or not? Sy, I do graunt that he did ope it. Ioi. But what neadeth this reseration or openyng, if the soules doo not entre in to lyfe? Where as notwithstādyng Paul doeth say: I coueit to be dissolued, & deliuered from this body, & to be w chrift. beleuyng that after this death, he should be with Christ. Peter moreouer doeth saye, that for this cause, the gospel was preached vnto the dead, that they shuld be iudged in the flesh, but lyue, after, or in y spirit, do not these manifest places teache & proue, that the soules doo lyue, with God? For he sayeth that y gospell was preached vnto the dead. What is els the gospel, to be preached, but redemption & lyfe to be preached. And what were they that were dead, but they,

they, which after that thei were
departed, were gathered in the
bosome of Abraham? Sy. But
howe was the gospell preached
vnto them? Ioia. The vertue of
the passion of Christ, and the
fruit of his death, which were
profitable vnto them. Sy. How?
Ioi. Because that they being de=
liuered, thorough the death of
Christ, ar receiued, as touching
their soules, into euerlastyug
lyfe. In the last day, they shall
ryse bodily, and as all other,
shall be iudged, in the vniuer=
sall iudgement. In the meane
season their soules do liue with
God. Is it proued sufficiently
that the soules that wer in the
bosome of Abraham are dely=
uered, & brought in to heauen?
Sy. I dooe not saye agaynst it.
Ioia. And thou shalt fynde none

D.ii. other

other thing in the worde of god. It followeth therfore, that the Bosome of Abraham is no dormitory, or slepyng place, but an euerlastyng lyfe: Which thyng we may proue by the .xvi. of Lu. For ther it is written, that Lazarus is in ioy and solace, wher as the rycheman is punysshed in hell. If so be that the soule, (as ye doo say) shulde slepe, she coulde haue no ioye, excepte it were by dreames: if she reioyseth or haue ioy, it is impossible that she shoulde slepe. Likewise it is manifestli knowen & shewed in the .viii. of Mathew, that many shall come, & sytte in the kyngdome of God, with Abraham, Isaak, and Jacob. That in the meane season, I shoulde sai nothing, that slepe is cleane contrarye to the nature of the soule

the Anababtistes.

soule, which is in Greke called Entelecheia, or Endelechia, that is to sai a perpetuall and vnrequietable motion or workyng. Sy. These thinges are more manifest, and more strong, then I thought. Ioia. It is the poynte of an vnwise man to say, I thought not, and hauyng hearde, but one parte, to geue sentence. The Anababtistes do aduaunce, and set forth gaily, and paintyngly their argumentes, but they are weake and nothyng strong.

Sy. I woulde fayne know, in what significaciō, the scripture vseth this worde to slepe, which is so often tymes founde, in euery place of the Bible. Ioia. Among the auncient fathers, this worde, to slepe, was to dye naturally, or after the commen course of nature. And because of the of the resurrectiō, it was saied, that thei which dyd dye, sleape. For as a man geueth hym selfe to sleape, doubting nothing, but that he shall wake agayne from his sleape: so the body sleapeth, that is to say dyeth, & doeth lye in the graue, beyng kepte there, tyl the day of the general resurrection. So the Fathers dyd sleape: so Stephen, & all other godly persons. Seyng therfore that to sleape, is to dye, and the soules can not dye, it foloweth, that they canne not sleape. For Stephen dyd saye: Lorde, receiue thou my spirite, whiche thyng: when he had saied, & had cōmitted or cōmended his soule to the heauenly father, his body sleapynge, dyd dye. In thys thyng, they are deceyued, that they do attribute vnto the soule

that

that which belongeth to the body only. But in the meane seasō it is attributed to the whole mā because of the vnitie of the body and of the soule, beyng knytted in one persone. Which example was brought afore, of Christ, in whom the body dyed only, & not his godhead, nor his soule. Lykewyse a man slepeth, but with his bodye, & not with his soule. The Anababtistes doo not, nor wyl not vnderstand this figure sinecdoche, nor the other figures, & tropes. Which thyng causeth them to erre in many thynges. But ignoraūcye maketh them the bolder, to teache, what so euer they do dreame or conceyue in their sleape. Sy. Yet it is euident that Paul saith, that a coroune of rightwisnes shalbe rē-
dered vn-

vnto him at lengthe, when the Lorde cometh. And also that, which is written in John, and in the Epistle to the Philipens. is sure and strongly grounded. Iois. This ought to be obserued Symon, that the daye of the Lorde in scriptures, is not alwayes to bee taken for the last Day, but somtyme, for the truthe and lyght: as in the gospell of John, otherwhyles for the visitacion of the Lorde: as often tymes, in the Prophetes, and .i. Cor. iii. sometyme for the ende & death of euery man: as John vi. I wyll resussitate or rayse him agayne, to euerlastyng life, in the last daye, that is to saye, when he dyeth. For when any man dyeth, that day is last vnto hym. After thys maner, dyd Paule call, the last daye, in the Epistle

Epistle to Timothe. For he had spoken before of his death, saiyng: I am ready to be offered: affirming, that he had ben faithfull and loyall, in his course, & therfore, he dyd not doubte, but that the rightwise iudge, shulde render vnto him, the coroune of rightwysnesse, which, as he leaueth no vnrightwysnesse vnpunyshed, so alwayes rewardeth them that labor faithfully. And this place doeth rather for vs, then for the Anababtistes, seing that Paule dothe hope, that the coroune of rightwysnesse, duyd vnto the rightwyse, shalbe renderyd vnto him, at the tyme of his death. Ergo, he beleueth not, that the soules do slepe, but that they do lyue euerlastingly. That, which thou aledgest out of John and Paule to the Philipenses,

lipenses, are spoken, of the last iudgement, but they proue not that the soules are a sleape. For that, whiche they doo speake of saluation there, dooe perteyne more to the resurrection of the body. For these are the wordes of Paule: He shall transforme (that is to say Christ) our vyle body, that he may make it conforme and lyke, to his glorious body. What meane these things elles, but that our bodyes haue full hope of resurrection, or rising agayn? As Iob dyd speke Iob.ix. Sy. If the soules dooe receyue by and by, their iudgement as sone, as they be departed, what neadeth that vniuersall iudgement? Ioia. It perteyneth to the whole man, whiche shall be repayred or made new agane, with the body, that

shall

the Anababtistes.

shall ryse, & with the soule. Of the which thyng, it is written, Thess. iiii. & Mat. xxiiii. & xxv. Doest thou yet desyre any thig?

Sy. I had leauer heare foundations and groundes oute of the scriptures. Ioia. I haue brought verye many already, what dooest thou aske more?

Sy. Thou hast other helpes yet, the which I pray the, to bryng forth. Ioi2. Seynge that thou arte desyrous of the truthe, I wyll hyde nothyng frome the. This Doctrine and Opinion, of the Sleape of the Soules, dooeth not ouelye repugne agaynst the Scriptures & fayth, dooeth not onely disanulle the Gospell aud Resurrection of Christ, but is also agaynst all comune sense & reasone, a rude and vnclearkelye ignoraunce,

but

but go to, let vs expounde these thynges: I aske thee, if the soule be a body, or a spirite? Sy. It is not a bodye, nor any grosse substaunce, but a syngle and pure spirite. Ioia. Can then a spirite be subiect to bodily infirmities, as to be an hongered, to be weryed, to dye. &c. Sy. No, for these perteyne to the bodye onely. A spirite, is immortall, incorruptible, euerlasting or perpetuall. Ioiada. Thou sayest very well, therfore marke thyne argumēt thus: Sith the soule is a spirit, & not a bodye, it can not be subiecte to bodily passions or infirmities, but is exempte frome them: slepe doth chaunce to the body, thorough werinesse. Ergo the soule can not slepe: for the soule cannot be weary. Or canst thou brynge any other thynge concer-

the Anababtistes.

concernyng slepe? Sy. No, for all operacions and senses dooe cease and rest, and excepte the body shulde brethe, folkes wold thynke that it were dead. Ioia. Now, if our soules should slepe, it shulde folow, that after this lyfe, we doo feele neither good, nor euyll, which dothe directly pugne agaynste the Gospell. Moreouer, we wyl proue by the nature of the slepe, that the soules can not slepe, but the bodye only. For now I aske the, when doeth the soule slepe, after that she is departed frome the body, or when she is yet ioyned to the body? Sy. At bothe tymes. Ioi. Neither of them can be trew: and I do meruail that so grosse an answere dyd come from the. For seyng that the Soule, can muche lesse slepe, when she hath
put

put awaye the burdeyn of the body, then when she beareth about yet, the burdeyn of the body, & doeth not sleape, when she is yet in the bodye, it followeth that she sleapeth muche lesse, when she is deliuered from the bodye. And that she doeth not slepe beyng in the body, it maye be knowen by thys, that in the tyme of wakyng, the body doth alwayes, without rest & quyet, worke, which actions do come from the soule. Ergo, it is manifest, that whiles that the body waketh, the soule sleapeth not. And agayn, when the body hath gent it self to rest & to slepe, the soule worketh with a perpetual motion or monyng, & doeth neuer rest or cease, either she bretheth, or doeth some thynge alwayes, withe the vertue of rememmembraunce & vnderstādyng, or with the other excellent vertues & powers. All mans lyfe is eyther wakynge, or rest: in none of them bothe, doeth the soule sleape. Ergo the soule doeth not sleape at all. Therfore slepe, longeth only to the body, & not to the soule. For when the soule begineth ones to haue life it is a perpetual Entelechia, comeyng frō the euerlasting & eternall fontayne of goodnesse, the which perpetuall Entelecheia, that is to say, vnrequietable, & perpetuall action and mouyng in the soule, if any man denayeth, by that same reason he must denay the soule Sy. These thyngz are somewhat darke vnto me. Ioiada. Therefore, J wyll declare them, by an exāple: Fyer is a very pure & actuall thyng, which

whiche after that it begynneth
ones, can neuer ceasse from his
operacion and workyng, tyll it
be quenched: and that is, when
it hathe nothyng, wherbpon, it
maye shew, and exercise his o-
peracion. If thou denyest the o-
peracion & working of the fier,
thou hast denyed the fyer. The
nature of the soule is very like,
which after, that she is poured
into the body, by god, is a liuely and working spirite, and can
neuer ceasse nor be at rest. Wylt
thou haue no fyer, take awaye
the operacion. If thou denyest
the Soule, attribute vnto her,
slepe. For to say, that the soule
is a slepe, and to saye, that the
soule is not, is all one thyng.
If the soule slepeth, she dooeth
rest, if she dooeth rest, she worketh not, if she doeth not worke,
she is

the Anabaptistes.

she is not. For to worke, and to be in the soule, is all one thing, syth that she is a perpetual motion, & workyng. But the soule is, therfore shee sleapeth not. Dooest thou vnderstande this thyng? Sy. Very well. Ioia. Therfore did I say, that the Anabaptistes knowe not, the nature of the soule. Sy. Thou shuldest peraduenture haue persuaded somewhat, to Timeus, and Phedrus, Platos disciples, I had leauer heare Scriptures. Ioia. The Saduces, dyd teache that ther was no Resurrection, and by this, dyd denye the immortalitie, and perpetual workyng of the soule, yea, and also Angels, and all maner of Spirites. Act. xiii. The Lorde dyd stop their mouthes, with these reasons. Ye erre (sayth he) not knowing the scriptures, nor the vertue of God. God, after the death of the Fathers, calleth hym selfe, the God of Abraham, Isaac and Jacob, which is not the God, of the dead. but of the lyuyng, and that therfore, Abraham, and the other Fathers were alyue, and not dead. Thei were dead in body, a gret whyle afore, and buryed: Therfore Christ speaketh here, of the lyfe of the soule. Ergo, the soule beyng separated from the body, is in her owne kynde, worketh lyuely, and slepeth not. This syllogysme and argument, doo I put to all the Anabaptistes, to answer to, that they may cleare them selfe frome the heresye of the Saduces. For thei are lyke vnto the Saduces and Manicheans. What shoulde I say of the

the wordes of Christ, whiche hangyng vpon the Crosse, doeth comforte, the thiefe with these wordes, saiyng: To daye thou shalte be with me in Paradise.

Sy. Paradise, and the Bosome of Abraham, are all one thyng, to the Anababtistes, where thei say, that the soules doo sleape.

Ioia. Thei do affirme this without scriptures, and with an hereticall spirite. Christ sayeth: To day, thou shalte be with me in Paradise. Ponder euerye worde. If Paradice, is a sleapyng place, Christ sleapeth in it also. For he sayeth: To daye thou shalte be. Moreouer, the thiefe prayeth Christ, to remember him, when he shoulde come in to hys kyngdome. If the kyngdome of God, is a Dormitorie or Sleapyng place: what

P.ii.   doo

doo the scriptures speake, of the Resurrection, and Ascendyng of Christ in to heauen? Ye are obstacle asses, O Anababtistes, whiche dare make mention of suche sleapyng, agaynst so manifest places of the scriptures. What shall they say, to the wordes of Christ. John. v. He that heareth my word, and beleueth in him, that hath sent me, shall not come in to iudgement, but is passed frome deathe to lyfe. Whiche woordes are so cleare, that no mā can denay them, but heretikes. Let the. xi. of John. and the. xv. of the first Epistle to the Corinthians. Item the .ii. Cor. ii. be reade, and it shal euidently be knowen, that the sleape of the Anababtistes, is a blasphemy agaynst the Gospell and Resurrection of Christ.

Sy.

Sy. If the matter be better looked vpon: the Anabaptistes can not cleare them selues, from the crime of ouer boldnesse & ignorancye: but they haue not pondered all these thingſ so exactly Ioia. Why dooe they presume to teach then, & take vpō thē that, which passeth their strengthe? And agayne, when they be conuicted, wyll not geue the vpper hande to the truthe? But because they wyll be sene stedfast, they be founde, in all thynges, frowarde, and obstacle. To say briefly: They doo all thynges, with contention, arrogancye, and ignoraunce. Sy. I woulde had questioned with the, touchyng the .vi. Conclusion, but that I must go to myne Inne: To morow, if thou canst haue leasyr, I wyll be here betymes
in the

Against the Anabaptistes.

in the morning, and reason farther with the. Ioiada. I am well pleased, for I wyll go, to myne Inne also: be thou tomorow, in better readinesse.

symon. God be with the. Ioiada. Farewell.

SOLI DEO HONOR ET GLORIA.

¶ Thou shalt vnderstãde, good Christen Reader, that immediately after this, as sone as may be, thou shalte haue the seconde Booke, whiche entreate vpon as many thynges as this Booke doeth, bothe fruitfull to be knowen, and also most necessarye for these perillouse tymes: in the which, the Diuell doeth all, that he can, to extinguish the trew Doctrine of the Gospell: whiche at this tyme, thorough our godly Magistrates, doeth reuiue, and florish agayne: Fare well, and pray, that we may performe the Woorke that we haue in haude.

✠

(C.)

Imprintyd at London, by Humfrey
Powell, dwellyng aboue Hol-
burne Conduit.

Cum priuilegio ad impri-
mendum solum.

ANNO DO. 1548.